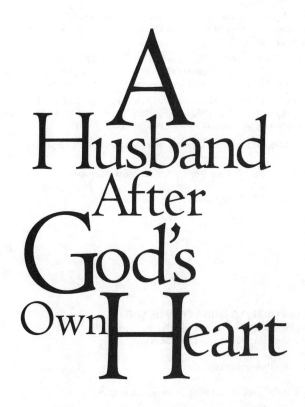

JIM GEORGE

HARVEST HOUSE PUBLISHERS

EUGENE, OREGON

Cover by Garborg Design Works, Minneapolis, Minnesota

Cover photo © William Faulder/Getty Images

A HUSBAND AFTER GOD'S OWN HEART
Copyright © 2004 by Jim George
Published by Harvest House Publishers
Eugene, Oregon 97402
www.harvesthousepublishers.com

Library of Congress Cataloging-in-Publication Data

George, Jim, 1943-
    A husband after God's own heart / Jim George.
        p. cm.
Includes bibliographical references.
    ISBN 0-7369-1166-9 (pbk.)
    1. Husbands—Religious life. 2. Marriage—Religious aspects—Christianity. I. Title.
    BV4528.2.G456 2004
    248.8'425—dc22   2003018822

Printed in the United States of America

05 06 07 08 09 10 11 /DP-KB/ 10 9 8 7 6 5 4 3

For Elizabeth,
my faithful life companion
and friend!

Contents

Becoming...A Husband After God's
Own Heart   7

1. Growing in the Lord   9

2. Working as a Team 25

3. Learning to Communicate 41

4. Enjoying Intimacy. 61

5. Managing Your Money. 77

6. Keeping Up the Home. 95

7. Raising Your Children. 111

8. Extending Love to Family. 127

9. Tending Your Career. 143

10. Making Time for Fun. 161

11. Serving the Lord 177

12. Reaching Out to Others 195

   Study Questions 213

   Notes. 231

Becoming...

A Husband After God's Own Heart

A *Husband After God's Own Heart* has been nearly 40 years in the making. Why? Because that's how long I've been developing as a husband. And now I have taken pen in hand in response to the many requests that have come my way—requests from both men and wives—asking me to address the specific and most important area of a married man's life, that of his relationship with his wife.

Marriage is a lot of work! But isn't it encouraging to know that God, the Creator of marriage, has already provided everything you need to fulfill His will and design for you as a husband? In this book we will look at...

> *...12 areas of your life as a husband*—what the Bible says about the areas that really matter to the health and vibrancy of your marriage. In addition, I've included...

> *...a list of "little things"* at the end of each chapter. These "little things" are designed to encourage, motivate, and guide you to work out the many

"little" ways you can practically fulfill your role as a husband.

...*a list of study questions* at the back of the book. These questions are written to enrich your personal knowledge and application of the biblical and practical truths shared throughout this book.

I invite you to join me in a journey down the path of comprehending and implementing God's desires for us as husbands. And to make this journey even more enjoyable, ask your wife to join in it with you and read along in her copy of my wife's companion book, *A Wife After God's Own Heart,* by Elizabeth George.

Friend and brother, no matter what your age or the state of your marriage today, and no matter what season of marriage you and your wife have entered, this book presents God's timeless guidelines for you as a husband. You can...

...read it before you marry

...read it alone to enhance your marriage

...read it together with your wife

...read it in a men's or couples' Bible study

...read it in your men's Sunday school class

...read it in your couples' Sunday school class

May God richly bless you as you continue growing as a Christian, in your faith, and in your understanding of what it means to be a husband after God's own heart!

1

Growing in the Lord

Seek first the kingdom of God and His righteousness,
and all these things shall be added to you.
MATTHEW 6:33

When I was a young boy, I couldn't wait to grow physically. At each phase of my early life, I wanted desperately to have the physical maturity to compete in sports at the next level...with the big boys! And even while I was at one particular point of growth, I exercised daily to develop my body to compete in sports at the next level.

On the other hand, when it came to growing in the mental area, I wasn't quite as motivated. My parents didn't have much formal education, so they were happy with whatever I accomplished in school. Surprisingly enough, with all of my efforts to succeed in the physical area, I ended up excelling in school in the mental arena.

And then there was the spiritual area of my life. I would like to report that my spiritual growth, which started when I was just six years old, was a magnificent upward spiral, and that it had few, if any, valleys. But no. Sad to say, my spiritual growth in those early years was an up-and-down roller coaster. And the downward drop on that roller coaster continued on into my early adult life and had a serious effect on my marriage.

I'll share more about my spiritual growth and the how-to's of growing in the Lord throughout this chapter, but for now, I want to make the statement (and I'm sure you will agree) that spiritual growth takes even more effort than physical growth.

It's true that spiritual development takes terrific effort. But, my friend, it's also true that the rewards are great, especially when it comes to being a husband...and that's what this book is all about. I want us to note how growing in the Lord occurs, and how that growth gives essential help for you and me for our life in general and our marriage and family in particular.

And keep this in mind as you read: No matter how old you are or how long—or short!—you've been married, the day you accelerate your growth in the Lord is the day your marriage is positively impacted, improved, and strengthened!

First Things First

If you're like most men and husbands, you're probably extremely busy. You're out there in the world every day, working and slaving away. Then, when you get home, more work awaits you—the work of taking care of your home and finances. And if you have children, you get home only to switch hats and try to be a good dad. With all these responsibilities, it's easy to conclude that there just isn't any time for growing spiritually.

Well, my new friend, that's why we want to start our study of what it means to be *A Husband After God's Own Heart* with this most strategic topic. Why?

Spiritual growth determines priorities. Spiritual growth is the key to all that's important in your life. That's what Jesus meant 2000 years ago when He told a listening audience not to be anxious about life and living. He said, "Do not worry, saying, 'What shall we eat?' or 'What shall we drink?' or 'What shall we wear?'" (Matthew 6:31). These things are definitely needful, but they are not what's really important. They are not your first priority.

What *is* really important is your spiritual growth. Why? Jesus went on to say that instead of worrying about the necessities of daily life, you should "seek first the kingdom of God and His righteousness, and *all these things* shall be added to you" (verse 33). In other words, *you* are to seek a life of spiritual growth and following after God's priorities for your life. Then, friend, *God* will provide for you and your family. That's God's promise! Seek God...and have everything! Seek the world...and lose everything (Luke 9:25). The right choice seems pretty obvious, doesn't it?

> Put first things first
> and we get second things thrown in:
> Put second things first
> and we lose both first and second things.[1]

Spiritual growth promotes purity. Besides determining a man's priorities, spiritual growth also promises help in the area of purity. In Psalm 119:9 the psalmist asked the question, "How can a young man keep his way pure?"

(NASB). Of all the questions men ask me, most of them deal with the area of purity. With all that is going on in our world today, Christian men are having a hard time staying pure, thinking pure thoughts, and developing pure habits.

But this is not new. Temptation and sin have been around since the beginning of history. God knows the struggles we face. In fact, God faced those same issues first-hand in the person of His Son, Jesus Christ (Hebrews 2:17-18). And God says we can have victory. How? In the psalm I just shared, the psalmist answered his question on purity in the same verse with this advice, "By taking heed according to Your word" (verse 9). Victory is ours if and when we heed God and His Word. So spiritual growth—through prayer, study of the Bible, and obedience—is the answer. Again, the psalmist follows up his earlier question of purity with this answer: "With my whole heart I have sought You; oh, let me not wander from Your command-ments! Your word I have hidden in my heart, that I might not sin against You" (Psalm 119:10-11).

Do you struggle with purity? If so, you are not alone. The Bible says that temptations are "common to man" (1 Corinthians 10:13). No man is immune to sexual temp-tation or a myriad of other kinds of temptations (verse 12). But there's hope!

Continuing on in 1 Corinthians 10, the Bible reports that God has provided a way of escape (verse 13). And what is the way of escape? Answer: Growing in the Lord and His grace! The process of growing in the Lord exposes us to the spiritual resources that we have been given to fight the battle and gain the victory in the areas of our struggle, whether it's with physical temptations like lust, or with other kinds of temptations like pride, greed, or anger.

Let's not be like the rich man I read about in the news-paper who died of starvation. He had all the resources needed to live well, but he was too stingy to use some of those resources and therefore starved to death. God has provided the resources for you, my friend. Make it your business to find out what those resources are. Then use them to gain the victory in the battle for purity.

Spiritual growth produces discernment. As we move through this book, I will talk constantly about leader-ship—leadership as a husband, leadership as a parent, leadership in the many areas of your life. God's husband knows where he is going. God's husband also knows how to get there, and he is able to guide his wife and children. How is this possible? Because God's kind of husband has God's wisdom and discernment.

Where does a Christian man get this wisdom and dis-cernment? I think you know the answer—from God's Word. And why is spiritual wisdom important? "That we should no longer be children, tossed to and fro and carried about with every wind of doctrine, by the trickery of men, in the cunning craftiness of deceitful plotting" (Ephesians 4:14). Our wives, our families, and our churches need godly men who have discernment—discernment to deal with life and life-issues on a spiritual level. That maturity comes as we grow in "the knowledge of the Son of God, to a perfect man, to the measure of the stature of the fullness of Christ" (verse 13). Such maturity is called *Christlike-ness,* which means to live and act as Christ lived and acted.

> Growing in the Lord is essential for becoming a man of right priorities, a man of purity, and a man of spiritual perception.

Not only do we need discernment for understanding the Bible, but we also need wisdom for the everyday decisions we must make as husbands, fathers, employees, and employers. Again, spiritual maturity is the answer. The writer to a group of Jewish Christians in the first century laments over their lack of growth. Hear his disappointment:

> For though by this time you ought to be teachers, you need someone to teach you again the first principles of the oracles of God; and you have come to need milk and not solid food. For everyone who partakes only of milk is unskilled in the word of righteousness, for he is a babe (Hebrews 5:12-13).

God is speaking to you and me today through this same text, and He is just as concerned today with our maturity as He was 2000 years ago with those readers. We as Christian husbands need to be teachers of spiritual things—if not verbally, then at least with our lives.

How does one remedy a lack of maturity? How does one gain the maturity needed to make wise and godly decisions?

The inspired writer goes on again to give us the answer:

> Solid food belongs to those who are of full age, that is, those who by reason of use have their

senses exercised to discern both good and evil (verse 14).

Growing in the Lord is essential for becoming a man of right priorities, a man of purity, and a man of spiritual perception. I pray that you have long ago recognized this fact and are well on your way along the road to maturity. When I think of you, I feel like the apostle John when he wrote to his readers, "I have no greater joy than to hear that my children walk in truth" (3 John 4). But if you haven't been aware of your need to grow in the Lord, I hope and pray that you have at least had your eyes opened to the absolute necessity of spiritual growth.

Deciding to Grow

One of my favorite men of the Old Testament is Joshua. Why him? Well, he was a great man who made the right choices in important decisions throughout his lifetime. For instance,

∽   Joshua was a man of great humility. He made a decision early on in his life to nurture the heart of a servant. How could he not be humble? After all, he was Moses' understudy for 40 years. This was the Moses whom God described as "very humble, more than all men who were on the face of the earth" (Numbers 12:3). And Joshua was called the servant of Moses (Numbers 11:28).

∽   Joshua was a man of great courage. Talk about "peer pressure"! Joshua made a decision to go against popular opinion and, along with Caleb, gave a positive report about the Promised Land that the Israelites were told to enter, giants and all (Numbers 14:6-9)!

∽ Joshua was a man of great faith. He made a decision to trust in God's ability to defeat the people inhabiting the Promised Land. Ten of the men who were sent to spy out the land came back with stories of "giants" and pictured themselves as "grasshoppers" next to these giants. Joshua and Caleb, however, had faith in God and declared, "If the Lord delights in us, then He will bring us into this land and give it to us" (Numbers 14:8)! Joshua's decision, shared by Caleb, earned them the privilege of being the only men of their generation to enter the Promised Land. All the others had weak faith and chose poorly. God reports that Joshua "wholly followed the LORD" (Numbers 32:12).

∽ Joshua was a man of great integrity. Even toward the end of his long life of service, Joshua was still making decisions for himself and for his family to serve the Lord, and not the false gods that surrounded them. And with the strength of his great faith, he called others to commit themselves to the same standard as well. Joshua exhorted, "Choose for yourself this day whom you will serve" (Joshua 24:15).

I think you can see why Joshua was such a key figure in the Old Testament and why I admire him so much. He was constantly making the hard decisions—the right decisions—decisions to serve God and not follow after the world and its allurements.

You and I need to respond to Joshua's challenge to "choose today whom you will serve." And don't fail to notice that Joshua, as the leader of a nation, included his family in his commitment: "As for me and my house, we will serve the LORD" (verse 15). My friend, Joshua's resolve needs to be ours as well. Again, growing in the Lord will help strengthen your resolve to be a godly husband who will stand up in the midst of an evil society and declare his commitment to lead his family away from the world, toward God, and into service to God. Perhaps this is a good time to ask God to give you Joshua's resolve as you read my personal prayer of commitment. May it be yours as well!

Dear God in heaven—the God who blessed Joshua for the decisions he made to honor and follow You—may this be a new beginning for me. May I resolve that, as of today, my life will better reflect Thee...that I will seek Your righteousness with my whole heart...that I will make a daily commitment to grow in my relationship with Your Son, my Savior, the Lord Jesus Christ. Dear Lord, my desire is to be a husband who leads by example, loves sacrificially, and serves selflessly. May I become a husband after Your own heart. Amen.

Reaping God's Blessings

I recently read a quip that suggested, "If you don't like what you are reaping, change what you are sowing." Perhaps you know that some things aren't quite right in your home. You know that somehow your spiritual growth (or lack thereof) is connected with what's not quite right in your life and marriage. But, with all the pressures of family and job, you can't seem to "fit in" growing in the Lord. So you struggle on.

Friend, I just described my life in years past. I was sowing selfishness and personal gratification. I was living a life of personal ambition. My goal was to be a highly successful executive for a big company. I was off doing my own thing, and, believe me, God was not part of the equation! And my life and my marriage were reaping frustration and disappointment. My wife was even on the verge of leaving me.

But then a change came. By God's grace, we became a Christian couple. Ours became a Christian marriage. With God's help I began to change what I was sowing, so to speak. And I have to say, it wasn't easy. One day I would sow a bag of good seed. The next day the bag was full of bad seed. But I desired to grow, and I sought help. I found men who could disciple me and show me what it means to be a husband after God's own heart. Slowly I stopped living a life of selfishness and personal gratification and started to more and

> God will bless you and your marriage when you follow His blueprint.

more consistently live for Jesus Christ. As I was growing in the Lord and learning how to love my wife, God began to bless. And He blessed, as Ephesians 3:20 says, "exceedingly abundantly above all that we ask or think"!

Marriage is a great invention of God. And a marriage where the husband desires to love his wife as Christ loved the church is a true witness to the reality of the Christian faith. But a marriage that honors Jesus Christ is not easy to come by. If you want this kind of marriage, then, like me, you are going to have to work at it.

God wants to bless you and your marriage. And, brother, God will bless you and your marriage when you follow His blueprint. I trust you have made some significant commitments while reading this chapter. And I pray you have committed to growing in the Lord. That's where you and I must start. It will require work, but oh, the blessings that await you!

How's Your Heart?

You may or may not have read my book *A Man After God's Own Heart*,[2] but in that book I constantly challenge the man reading it to check his heart. The title of that book was taken from God's description of King David as found in Acts 13:22. David wasn't always the man he should have been, but deep down in his heart, God could see that he had a desire to follow after Him.

I'm going to now pick up where I left off in *A Man After God's Own Heart* and ask that same question again. *How's your heart?* Do you truly want to grow spiritually? Do you want to follow God and His commands for your life? These are hard questions, but they must be asked...and they must be answered. It's critical right now to stop and answer. Is your answer yes or no?

You may want to say yes, but perhaps you are thinking, *I can't live that kind of perfect life! I've tried, and I end up stumbling and falling. I can't be perfect.* Well, brother, relax! I'm not talking about perfection. David wasn't perfect, and I'm not perfect. In fact, no man is perfect (Romans 3:23). The only man who was perfect is Jesus Christ, the Son of God (Hebrews 4:15). No, what I am talking about is progression. Yes, like David, you and I stumble and fall at times. Yet God's man—God's husband—gets up off the deck when he's fallen, seeks forgiveness, and moves on. Even though you might go two steps forward and one step back, that's still progression! And that's spiritual growth!

Once again, how's your heart? I believe you do have a heart for God and the things of God. And I believe you want to be a husband after God's own heart. I know I do. So together, let's keep moving through this book. And together, let's keep growing spiritually so we too can grow to "the measure of the stature of the fullness of Christ" (Ephesians 4:13).

In the next several pages we are going to continue looking at this vital topic of growing in the Lord as we consider the "little things" you and I can do that will make a big difference in our marriage, but for now, remember...

when you grow in the Lord,
    you grow in your ability to be a godly husband,
        you grow in your ability to be a godly parent,
    and you grow in your ability to lead.
    So...

Seek first the kingdom of God and His righteousness,
and all these things shall be added to you.
MATTHEW 6:33

Little Things That Make a Big Difference

1. Read your Bible every day.

It's been calculated that if you read your Bible just ten minutes a day, you will read through it in one year. So decide on a time. Then pick a place. Start in Genesis 1:1 or Matthew 1:1. It doesn't matter where you start...as long as you start! The idea is to regularly and systematically read through your Bible. No other book can claim to be "living and powerful...a discerner of the thoughts and intents of the heart" (Hebrews 4:12). Allow God to work in your life and marriage as you read and meditate on His Word.

2. Go to church every week.

Obviously this isn't such a "little" thing because church is such a big part of the Christian life. Church is where you and your family can corporately worship God, learn biblical truth from gifted pastors and teachers, fellowship with other believers and couples, and minister your spiritual gifts. It's true you can worship God anywhere, but God has established the church so that we would worship Him somewhere (Hebrews 10:25). If you can make it to work five days a week, why can't you make it to church one day each week?

3. Visit a Christian bookstore.

Ask God, before you go into your local Christian bookstore, to show you which books would be helpful to you at this stage of your life and marriage. Then walk in and ask directions to the men's section for yourself and the marriage section for your marriage. Browse through the titles and prayerfully select those that attract your interest. Also, maybe it's time to upgrade your Bible with a study Bible that has explanatory notes in it. Or, if you have trouble understanding the language of your present Bible, find a translation that is a little more reader-friendly.

4. Seek out a mentor.

If you've ever had a personal trainer or coach, you know how helpful it was in your physical or business training. Well, a discipler or mentor can be just as helpful in your spiritual training. You know you should be growing spiritually, you know you should be improving in your marriage, but you are not quite sure how to get the job done. A mentor can help. Find someone who has gone before you, who is wise and mature in the things of the Lord and can help intensify your training as a Christian and as a husband. Remember, "Iron sharpens iron, so one man sharpens another" (Proverbs 27:17 NASB).

5. Sign up for a Bible class or Bible study.

God has given "pastors and teachers, for the equipping of the saints" in the church (Ephesians 4:11).

These men are gifted by God's Spirit and have studied and prepared to teach God's Word and assist you in your growth. Usually the size of a study group or class is small, which is less intimidating and gives you more freedom to ask questions. And to make your participation even more beneficial, why don't you and your wife sign up for a couples Bible class or Bible study together?

6. Pray for your wife.

Prayer is a spiritual discipline. When you pray, you are acknowledging that God is an active participant in your life. Taking time each day to pray will strengthen your spiritual life, which, in turn, will strengthen your marriage and have its greatest impact on your wife.

I think you will agree your wife is a busy lady. She wears a myriad of hats. She has a multitude of roles and responsibilities. And she is the major reason for any good thing that is happening in your life. So why shouldn't you pray for the growth, protection, and purity of the most special person in your life? Other than a godly mother, mother-in-law, or aunt, you might be the only person on the face of this earth who is praying regularly for your precious wife. Ask her for a photo. Then place it on your desk at work or near your computer. Whenever your eye catches a glimpse of her smiling face, remember to shoot up a prayer for whatever you know she is doing about that time of day.

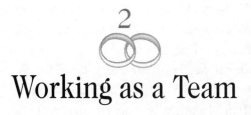

Working as a Team

Two are better than one,
because they have a good return for their work.
ECCLESIASTES 4:9 (NIV)

You may have noticed by now that I love sports! In fact, while growing up, I loved sports so much that I participated in a variety of them over the years. I was good at some...and not so good at others. But I still enjoyed playing with the guys. In most of those sandlot-type events, the teams were organized on the spot, and winning generally depended on which team had the best athletes. But sometimes winning occurred when a bunch of average guys played well as a team. (Do you relate? Does this bring back any of your childhood memories?)

Well, this principle about winning as a team is true in marriage as well: Marriage works best when a husband and wife work together as a team. That's the way God designed marriage. From the very beginning, God meant for the man and woman to work together. So let's start this chapter by looking at teamwork in marriage—God-style!

God's Winning Combination

The sports world has produced just a few of what I would call "perfect" teams. These are the teams that had "the winning combination." Because I'm not a sports historian, I can give only a limited perspective on which have been the most perfect teams in sports. But, which would you say were the best-of-the-best? In baseball? In football? In basketball? In other sports? In whatever sport you pick and whatever team you pick, this team put it all together. Some of these teams were loaded with talent. Others probably didn't have lots of players with the greatest talent, but they had the heart. They worked as a team and won it all.

In the Bible we also see the winning combination—God's "perfect team." This team was perfect because the God of perfection created it. Let's take a closer look at this team in Genesis 1 and 2 and see what we can learn from God's winning combination, God's perfect team, God's perfect marriage:

> ∞ *The team had the right owner*—In sports, the owner of the team plays a vital role in the success of the team. In this case, God, the creator and owner of this team, played the most important role of all. He formed this team from scratch. "The earth was without form, and void" (Genesis 1:2). "Then God said, 'Let Us make man in Our image, according to Our likeness'" (verse 26).

> ∞ *The team had the right coach*—Even the best of teams needs a good coach, one who can give strong direction. God provided such leadership, declaring, "Let them have dominion over the fish

of the sea, over the birds of the air, and over the cattle, over all the earth and over every creeping thing that creeps on the earth" (verse 26).

≈ *The team had members of equal nature and ability*—Can you imagine a team with everyone having equal natural talents and abilities? A team of Michael Jordans? God's team had two members who were created in the same image. Both were created in the image of God. "God created man in His own image; in the image of God He created him; male and female He created them" (verse 27).

≈ *The team had the right mandate*—To be a winning team, you need to know who your opponent is and what the strategy for winning is. And sometimes you need a good "half-time pep talk"! God's perfect marriage team had the gauntlet laid down for them. This was their game strategy: "Be fruitful and multiply; fill the earth and subdue it; have dominion over the fish of the sea, over the birds of the air, and over every living thing that moves on the earth" (verse 28).

≈ *The team had the right resources*—In some sports, equipment is everything. For instance, as a golfer, can you imagine having only one club in your bag? But not so with God. God said, "See, I have given you *every* herb that yields seed which is on the face of all the earth, and *every* tree whose fruit yields seed; to you it shall be for food" (verse 29). God's team had everything it needed to play the game of life.

∽ *The team had the right leader*—Whether in sports or business, one person must be in charge—one CEO, one quarterback, one point guard. In the case of God's team, the man was placed in this role of leadership. He was created first when "the LORD God formed man of the dust of the ground, and breathed into his nostrils the breath of life; and man became a living being" (Genesis 2:7). He was to name the animals. The woman was "brought" to him (verse 22), and he was the one who named her. From every possible angle, we see that the man was the central player on the team.

> You can make your marriage a little bit of heaven on earth by following God's plan of teamwork.

∽ *The team members understood their roles*—Man was the team leader. But God, the Owner-Coach, decided that rather than have the man try to do the job by himself, he could use a "helper," a wife, one who would support and assist him. God said, "It is not good that man should be alone; I will make him a helper comparable to him" (verse 18). This didn't make the wife any less of a player. No, as we've already seen, woman was created with the same image and nature as the man. She was "comparable" to the man (verse 18), his counterpart, equal in standing…but with a different role to play on the team. Theirs was to be a leader-helper relationship.

∽   *The team members lived out their roles*—It's one thing to know your role, but quite another to live it out. Let's say, for instance, that on my sandlot team I was assigned the role of tackle on the team, but in my heart I really wanted to play quarterback. This would definitely create a problem! But on God's team, we assume that Adam knew his role and functioned in it. And being the perfect team, we also assume the woman knew and functioned perfectly in her role.

Well, there you have it. Take a good, long look at the perfect team—the perfect marriage. We don't know how long God's team functioned as the perfect team because the Bible doesn't say. But we do know that, however long it lasted, it was heaven on earth! Just think of the best day you and your wife ever had together. No arguments. No disagreements. Nothing but harmony the whole day long. Then…imagine *every* day being like that, and, brother, you have a glimpse of that first marriage and that perfect relationship between husband and wife.

How can a marriage be a little bit of heaven on earth? Or more specifically, how can *your* marriage be a little bit of heaven on earth? Answer: By following God's plan of teamwork. Read now what Gary Thomas says about viewing your marriage as a team effort:

> When a man and woman marry, they are
> pledging to stop viewing themselves as individ-
> uals and start viewing themselves as a unit, as a
> couple. In marriage, I am no longer free to
> pursue whatever I want; I am no longer a single
> man. I am part of a team, and my ambitions,
> dreams, and energies need to take that into
> account.[3]

I think both you and I can see that we need to put away
selfishness and "childish things" (see 1 Corinthians 13:11)
and take on the concept of *team*-work and being a *team*
player!

Following God's Plan

I was just a young boy living in Oklahoma when it happened—we had just bought our first television! Immediately my dad and I sat down on that fateful Saturday to
watch OU (Oklahoma University, the "Boomer" Sooners)
play Notre Dame. The day is forever etched in my mind as
the day OU's winning streak—47 games without a loss—
ended. (And, if I'm not mistaken, that streak still holds the
record.) What happened? How could they lose? I'm sure
there were many reasons, such as, perhaps they played
against a better team. Whatever the reason, the winning
streak was over. And that was devastating news for every
OU fan.

Well, there was another winning streak that ended one
day, and men and women have never been the same since
that "loss" either. That was the day the perfect marriage
team suffered defeat. How did it happen? *First, the team
members were separated.* The woman was alone and

without her teammate and team leader, the man (Genesis 3:1). *Second, there was a formidable opponent.* "The serpent was more cunning than any beast of the field" (verse 1). *Third, the woman took on the opponent alone without her teammate* (verses 2-6). And as the saying goes, the rest is history! From the point of that first conniving attack and the ensuing defeat, the enemy, Satan, has been using the same successful strategy to attack and destroy marriages ever since. Witness now the breakup of that first perfect team and its results:

- ∞ The man blamed God and his wife—"The woman whom *You* gave to be with me, *she* gave me of the tree, and I ate" (verse 12).

- ∞ The battle of the sexes began—To the woman God said, "Your desire shall be for your husband, and he shall rule over you" (verse 16). One theologian interprets this verse in this way:

> Because of sin and the curse, the man and the woman will face struggles in their own relationship. Sin has turned the harmonious system of God-ordained roles into distasteful struggles of self-will. Lifelong companions, husbands and wives, will need God's help in getting along as a result. The woman's desire will be to lord it over her husband, but the husband will rule by divine design.[4]

But take heart! Not all is lost! Even though you and I are less-than-perfect people, we can again recapture a little bit of that original marriage's team-"form" if we will again take this theologian's advice and seek God's help and follow God's plan for our marriage by going back to the original plan—back to the basics.

Back to the Basics

Let's go back to that perfect team and see what it will take to regain that winning combination. I know at times I've failed to follow God's pattern for my marriage. How about you? Are you following the pattern of that original perfect team which was created and managed by God Himself? Let's ask ourselves some tough questions as we look at the basics again:

∽ *The team had the right owner*—Is God the owner of your marriage? The Bible says that every Christian has been bought with a price (1 Corinthians 7:23). That price is the death of Jesus Christ (1 Peter 2:24). Your team, made up of you and your wife, must start with the right owner. That's as basic as it gets! If Christ isn't the Lord of your life, this would be a good time to ask Him to be your Savior and thus come under new ownership. In case you are wondering what to do or how to make this "transaction," here is a prayer you can pray from your heart:

Jesus, I know I am a sinner, and I want to repent of my sins and turn and follow You. I believe that You died for my sins and rose again victorious over the power of sin and death, and I want to accept You as my personal Savior. Come into my life, Lord Jesus, and help me follow and obey You from this day forward. Amen.

∞ *The team had the right coach*—The Bible is God's rule book for life and for your marriage. How closely are you following God's rule book for your marriage? If you are not already reading your Bible on a daily basis, this would be a good day to start. You can't play the game successfully without knowing the rules. Find out what God, your coach, is asking of you.

∞ *The team had members of equal nature and ability*—How do you view your wife? Do you see her as second-class, as inferior? You might not come right out and admit such a view, but your actions may be revealing your heart, so check out your actions. God created your sweet wife in His image. In His eyes "there is neither male nor female; for you are all one in Christ Jesus" (Galatians 3:28). Therefore you are to treat your wife with the love and respect she deserves as an equal. In fact, if you gave her worth much thought, you might decide to call her your *better half*!

∞ *The team had the right mandate*—How do you see the mission of your marriage? You must realize that it is not to merely live together and/or have children. Obviously these are essential elements to any marriage, but the rest of the world does this. No, God has greater plans for you and your marriage. He has brought you and your wife together to serve Him, to "have dominion" and demonstrate His glory to a watching world. Why not sit down with your wife and draw up a "game plan" for glorifying God in your marriage?

∞ *The team had the right resources*—The Bible states that Jesus Christ "has given to us all things that pertain to life and godliness" (2 Peter 1:3). The resources for a God-honoring marriage are there. They're there, and they're available. Are you taking advantage of those resources "through the knowledge of Him who called [you]" (verse 3)?

∞ *The team had the right leader*—God has called you, the husband, to be the physical and spiritual leader in your marriage. How are you doing? Don't be discouraged if you're not quite where you need to be. But do ask God to give you a new resolve to be that leader. Ask Him to direct you to a man or men in your church who can help you to be that leader. Again, the resources are there. Don't be too proud to ask for help. Your team needs your leadership!

∞ *The team members understood their roles*—Do you and your wife have a good understanding of the role each of you is to play in your marriage? Again, make sure both of you look again at the rule book—the Bible—for a description of your

roles. Remember, marriage is a leader-helper relationship.

∾ *The team members lived out their roles*—As a
husband, you already know you can't make your
spouse live out her role as wife and helper, but you
(by God's grace) can live out God's role for you as
a leader in your marriage. Again, seek all the help
you can get to live out your role.

"Two Are Better than One"

King Solomon wrote the perfect words to sum up God's
view of teamwork in marriage. In the book of Ecclesiastes,
Solomon addressed many of life's issues, but in one particular section he wrote about the value of a companion,
or, in our case, a marriage companion. Read his wisdom,
and then let's remember it and apply it to our marriage.
Let's purpose to work as a team, and not merely as a team,
but a *winning* team!

Two are better than one,
because they have a good reward for their labor.
For if they fall, one will lift up his companion.
But woe to him who is alone when he falls,
for he has not one to help him up.
Again, if two lie down together,
they will keep warm;
But how can one be warm alone?
Though one may be overpowered by another,
two can withstand him.
ECCLESIASTES 4:9-12

God knows that "two are better than one." That's why He has given you your mate. Your wife is to be your companion—to live with, to love with, and together as a team, to conquer life's battles with.

Reaping the Blessings

In the Garden of Eden, God finished His perfect creation, and He blessed His first couple. They worked perfectly as a team, and theirs was a winning team. But now these many years later, after the fall into sin, God still desires to create new winning teams, and He wants to create such a team in *your* marriage. Why not follow His instructions and commit yourself to leading your wife and working as a team to fulfill God's plan for your marriage? Here are some of the blessings that will come with this kind of commitment:

> Follow God's plan and demonstrate to the watching world what a "winning team" looks like.

> *God will be honored*—What greater blessing can you enjoy than to exalt and honor God by honoring His design for your marriage?

> *Your marriage will be honored*—The world and even the Christian community is looking for marriages that work. Follow God's plan and demonstrate to the watching world what a "winning

team" looks like. Others will respect what they see and want to follow your godly model.

You will be complete—God's plan requires two people, a man and a woman, that will work together as a team, with each person enhancing the other. What a beautiful plan! Your weaknesses are enriched by your wife's strengths. In turn, your strengths supplement her weaknesses. So together, the two of you are a much stronger force for the cause of Jesus Christ. Now, *that's* glorious teamwork!

Little Things That Make a Big Difference

1. Plan together.

A team needs common goals and direction. Planning things together can give your marriage team that focus. So get together with your wife and pick a date when you can plan for next week and next month. Your objective is to work your way right on through the next year and on into the years to come. What else should you work on planning together? Your yearly vacation. Your children's education. Your retirement, etc. Once you both know the plan (whatever that might be), then you can both put all of your energies into fulfilling your plans...together.

2. Work together.

Your marriage is the union of two people who, when they work together as a team, can accomplish vastly more than when working separately. So select projects that allow you to work together to complete the task. Functioning as a team is not always easy. And you may have to work at it awhile until you are no longer working *against* each other, but *with* each other. Operating as a couple gets any job done faster, and you can have a lot of fun together in the process as well as the joy of mutual satisfaction as you admire your joint accomplishments.

3. Play together.

This "little thing" is so important we will devote an entire chapter to it (chapter 10, "Making Time for Fun"). But for now, realize that your marriage needs a break every so often. By that I mean a break from the stress of everyday living, working, raising children, doing household work. You need to plan a time when the two of you can have some fun. Hire a babysitter and have a night out. Do something that will take your mind off of other people and your pressures and allow you to focus on each other. Have some fun!

4. Pray together.

I mentioned praying *for* your wife in the previous chapter, but praying together *with* your wife takes prayer to another level. Carve out a time each day when the two of you can go to the Lord in mutual prayer. It doesn't have to be a long time, just a few minutes is good. Praying as a couple knits your hearts together for common spiritual concerns and direction. Your wife will hear your heart as you talk to God. And you will do likewise as you listen to her prayers. Your desires for your marriage will become fused with those of your wife as the two of you step out together in faith.

5. Think together.

While you will certainly cultivate friendships at work and at church, and have sports interests and hobbies that transcend your marriage, you must always think as a married man. Before you plunge into things, think "together" and ask for your wife's input and opinions. Let her know when your plans change and you won't be home on time. Consult her on a business venture, especially if it will affect her and your family financially. Try to abide by the Philippians 2:4 Principle: "Let each of you look out not only for his own interests, but also for the interests of others."

3

Learning to Communicate

Sweetness of the lips increases learning....
The heart of the wise teaches his mouth,
and adds learning to his lips.
PROVERBS 16:21,23

Give me a cup of coffee and I can ramble on for hours. Put me with my pastor-friends and we can discuss theology until the break of dawn. But sit me down with my wife...and sometimes there is deafening silence. Why does this happen? Why can't I be as expressive with my wife as I am with the guys at work?

It wasn't always this way. There was a time in our courtship when, with or without the coffee, Elizabeth and I could talk for hours. And during our engagement we could discuss anything and everything until the break of dawn. What terrible thing happened between courtship and marriage? What disease afflicted the two of us (or at least me) to the point where conversing with her became an effort? Was it amnesia, or memory loss? Was it that we had run out of things to talk about? Was it the loss of something between us? Or was it perhaps that I had simply quit trying?

Does this sound a little like your marriage? Do you recognize some bit of your situation in my story? It seems that communication—or the lack thereof—is a significant issue in most marriages. And it's no wonder that it's a problem if it's anything like one man's attempt to communicate—read on!

> With my date seated in front of me, I cleared my throat and began.
>
> "What did you say when you said what I thought you said? Did you say what you said when I thought you said your say?
>
> "Or have you said your say another way? What I meant to say was, what did you mean when you said what I thought you said? Did you mean what you said that day?
>
> "Okay, let me say it another way. What did you mean to say when you said what I think I thought you said, you know, when I thought you said your say the other day?"
>
> "I'm not sure," she replied.
>
> "Oh," I said.[5]

Now I must quickly add that my story isn't quite as bad as I portrayed it. And I don't think my ability to communicate with my wife is as confusing as the man in our example! But I do admit that communication is an area of my marriage that constantly needs help. And I'm sure I'm not alone in my need for help, either.

So, as we begin a new area of what it means to be a husband after God's own heart, you and I need to ask ourselves some soul-searching questions, such as...How can I regain that premarital glibness that my wife-to-be thought was so charming? How can I recapture the care with which I used to communicate my love and affection to my bride-to-be? And how can I improve my communication to the point where a few well-chosen words from me will be "like apples of gold in settings of silver" (Proverbs 25:11)?

"Like Apples of Gold"

Do you want your speech to be "aptly spoken" (Proverbs 25:11 NIV), like apples of gold? Imagine your words being so appropriate for every situation that your wife would value them as she would value a large mass of gold in the shape of an apple. That's what the writer of Proverbs is saying our words can be. With this picture of the value of exquisite speech in our minds, let's take the acrostic of S-P-E-E-C-H to heart—and regain all the wonderful communication that was so much a part of our marriage relationships in days gone by.

Swift in your listening—Listening is a lost art. Everyone, including you and me, is too impatient. We fail to respect the other person long enough to let them finish speaking before we jump in. We tend to value what *we* want to say more than we value the other person's words. Proverbs 18:2 has a special name for this kind of person— "A *fool* has no delight in understanding, but in expressing his own heart." Some people would call this one-way communication.

An inability to listen is a rampant problem in marriages. Have you ever been around a married couple only to listen to one or both of them interrupt the other with such "important" information as, "No, Harry, it wasn't six years ago, it was seven years!" "Excuse me, honey, but I think you're wrong. Bill didn't take a job in Cleveland, it was Chicago." Does this sound familiar? True communication is not a one-way street. Real communication requires that you first listen to what your wife is saying and then "fit" your words to communicate an appropriate response.

Then there is the husband who pretends he is listening when actually he's "tuned out." This is nothing but selfish preoccupation. He is so absorbed with his own life and issues that he just turns off his wife. He looks straight in her eyes yet his hearing goes blank. Most husbands, including you and me, are guilty on this count more often than we care to admit! Oh, we may nod at appropriate intervals, but we really aren't listening. This is actually disrespectful. When you or I tune our wife out, we are saying that her words, opinions, cares, concerns, and needs are not important.

I know that you value your wife and are concerned for her needs. That's why you're taking the time to read a book like this one. In times past you probably hung on every word that came out of her mouth. You listened intently for clues to better understand her. Clues to help you love her more. So what changed? Answer: *You* changed! Therefore, you must change again and rekindle your listening skills.

You must learn to "be swift to hear, slow to speak" (James 1:19)!

And while you're at it, listen to your wife's advice. God has given you a "second opinion" in your wife, so listen to her and take heed. As we have already seen, "Two are better than one" (Ecclesiastes 4:9). You'll be glad you did!

Prudent in your words—I would describe most men and their style of communicating as "the strong silent type." They are men of few words. Their communication consists of a lot of "yeps" and "nopes." But the principle of careful speech remains the same whether we speak with few or many words. We need to be mindful about what we say. Proverbs puts it this way: "In the multitude of words sin is not lacking, but he who restrains his lips is wise" (10:19). Let's not be silent. Our wife needs our input. Communication is a two-way street. But let's also be careful in what we say...and how we say it.

> *How* you speak is often more important than *what* you say!

Empathetic in your voice—When Elizabeth and I were first married, there were two hot topics we couldn't discuss without getting into a big argument—religion and politics. Then, miracles of miracles, God came into our marriage and religion was the *only* thing we wanted to talk about! How about you and your wife? Are there any hot topics or "buttons" that you or your wife push or avoid that cause the two of you to raise your voices at each other? Are there any topics or buttons that are certain to quickly erupt into a heated argument? If that's the case, then first identify those hot topics or hot buttons right now and determine that, with God's help, you will not be the one who raises your voice.

Also determine, with God's help, that you won't be the one who gets angry. In one of the few verses where husbands are specifically mentioned, the Bible says, "Husbands, love your wives and do not be harsh with them" (Colossians 3:19 NIV). You are to love your wife, be the peacemaker, and heed this advice: "A soft answer turns away wrath, but a harsh word stirs up anger" (Proverbs 15:1). Bottom line? Speak softly. *How* you speak is often more important than *what* you say!

Edifying with your approach—Have you ever had the horrifying experience of hearing one of your children repeat to another child some less-than-wholesome statement that you've used around the house? And then come to realize that you weren't even aware that you were saying such less-than-edifying words?

Our last point on communication dealt with the *manner* of your speech—speak softly. This point now deals with the *material* you speak. Take the Bible's advice when it comes to the character of your words: "Let no corrupt word proceed out of your mouth, but what is good for necessary edification, that it may impart grace to the hearers" (Ephesians 4:29).

Calming every issue—Imagine going to a boxing match. One man is in one corner wearing blue trunks, and the other fighter is in the opposite corner wearing red trunks.

The bell sounds...and only the man in the red trunks comes to center ring. Suddenly the fans begin to scream and yell when they realize there's no fight! Why? Because it takes two to have a fight.

It's the same in a marriage. Whenever there is an argument between you and your wife (notice I said *when*, not *if!*), be quick to ask for forgiveness. Be willing to be the first to say, "I'm sorry." Rather than be a part of the problem and contribute to the fight, practice "sweetness of the lips" (Proverbs 16:21). And what should you do if the argument's already begun? Answer: Be the first to ask for forgiveness. Seeking forgiveness is not an issue of who's right or wrong—it's an issue of obeying God. Jesus said, "If you...remember that your brother has something against you, leave your gift there before the altar, and go....be reconciled to your brother" (Matthew 5:23-24). So the wise husband calmly settles or ends the argument by asking for forgiveness.

Honoring the truth with your words—Great trust takes years to obtain...but can be lost instantly with the least of lies. If either you or your wife have ever been less than honest with each other, you know how long and hard it is to rebuild the resultant shattered trust! So you must always be honest in your communication with your wife. Don't say one thing when you really mean something else.

The religious leaders of Jesus' day were often guilty of deceptive speech. They would say one thing but really mean something else. Their deceptive speech came in many forms. That's why Jesus charged, "Let your 'Yes' be

'Yes' and your 'No,' 'No.' For whatever is more than these is from the evil one" (Matthew 5:37).

Friend, these words apply to us as well. We need to be straightforward and honest in our communication. And I would add, *especially* with your wife! Are you guilty of any of these forms of deceptive speech?

> An outright lie—and you know it
>
> An exaggeration—the old fish-that-got-away story
>
> A half or partial truth—such as when Abraham said his wife was his sister
>
> A skirting of the truth—evading or changing the topic to avoid answering the question

If so, follow the commands of Scripture by "putting away lying" and seeking to "speak truth" with your wife (Ephesians 4:25).

Well, there you have it. SPEECH that will honor God and your wife. What wife wouldn't respond positively to a husband who practiced this type of wise communication? And friend, your wife is no different. I often hear my wife talking to other wives who openly express their longing for their husbands to talk with them. Therefore I know there's more you and I can do in this area. So let's attempt to communicate our love to our wives more often and with better skills. And exactly where do we begin this process? We begin by taking the first step, which is summed up in one phrase—*loving* by understanding.

Loving by Understanding

Sigmund Freud, the "father" of psychoanalysis, made a statement something to this effect: After 40 years of practice he had yet to understand women. Do you ever feel that way about your wife? That the longer you live together the more of a mystery she becomes? Maybe that's why you love her so. You know, there's never a dull moment around the house! And just about the time you begin to figure her out, she changes!

Living with and loving your wife in an understanding way is a command to husbands from Scripture (1 Peter 3:7 NASB). How is this to be done? Through communication. But as we've already seen, communication is a significant problem for many couples. Why? Well, there are lots of reasons...as I can testify! In a moment I'll list for you just a few of the reasons husbands and wives have problems at times communicating with each other. These problems can be mutual. We can both fail to communicate for the same reasons or for different ones. And here's one thing I've learned: I can't work on my wife's communication problems, but I sure can work on mine! And just maybe, if I improve my ability to communicate, my wife will respond and communicate better. Then we both benefit from my effort. But regardless of what my wife does, God wants *me* to learn to better understand and support my wife.

So what are some hindrances to good communication? Here are a few. And feel free to add some of your own!

1. *Lack of time.* Good communication takes time. And time is one thing that seems to be so rare these days. With your hectic schedule—and your wife's, too—there just

doesn't seem to be enough time for solid, meaningful communication. Think for a moment about the amount of time you and your wife are alone together. Take yesterday as an example. Add up the minutes (not the hours) the two of you were awake and alone together. Was it five minutes in the morning and 15 minutes in the evening? If so, or if it's close, that's not much, is it? If that's the case, then no wonder the two of you are strangers living under the same roof. Hopefully you spend more time together than that.

2. *Lack of consideration.* Let's face it, you and I are basically selfish. We want *what* we want. And we want it *when* we want it! Our sin nature has created a self-centered preoccupation with self. Therefore we generally are not interested in our wife's day, her problems, her issues with the children, or her troubles at work. *We* have had a hard day! *We* deserve to be pampered and cared for. *We* are interested in coming home, having a nice meal, relaxing, and watching a little television. Never mind the fact that in many cases, your wife may have also put in an eight- or ten-hour day herself, and now she must come home and do all that's expected of the Proverbs 31 ideal wife and woman. A more considerate and loving husband would think of his wife (Philippians 2:3-4), and ask (that means *communicate!*) how he can help her end her day more easily.

3. *Lack of desire.* Here's the way it goes for me—If I want to go fishing, I find the time. If I want to jog, I find the time. You and I do what we want to do, don't we? If something is important to us and the desire is great enough, we do what it takes to accomplish it. Well, I trust that by now

you are understanding the importance of communication between you and your wife. Up to this time in your marriage, if you are like most men, you haven't put much effort into better communication with your wife because you haven't seen its importance.

Well, if you're a businessman, I know you would agree that communication is definitely important in the business world. When I was a salesman, I had to be able to communicate the superiority of my company's products. As a Bible teacher, I have to communicate accurately the truths of God's Word. And I'm sure good communication is important for you as well. Whether you are a salesman, an executive, an engineer, or whatever, you know you cannot be successful without good relational skills. So why not take some of this same motivation and drive that makes you successful in your job and apply it to communicating with your wife? The rewards will be much greater than any success you might have in a vocation. And besides, you will be fulfilling the Lord's command to live with your wife in an understanding way.

4. *Lack of common ground.* By "common ground" I mean common interests. Here's the scenario: At one time you were attracted to a young lady. When you got to know her a little better, you found out that the two of you had some of the same interests—perhaps music, hobbies, books, and hopefully, the Lord. You got married...and then things such as jobs, children, activities—you name it—began to wedge their way in between you and the person you earlier had all those things in common with. Now, years later into the marriage, you and your wife have

drifted apart. You are complete strangers. If nothing is done to remedy this, you and your wife will have nothing to say to each other for the next 20 years!

5. *Lack of energy.* When you're tired, it's easy to make excuses. And it's certainly easier to do nothing than to do something! You come home, slump down in your easy chair, and want to relax. You lamely justify your not wanting to communicate by thinking, *Since I'm tired and I've talked all day on my job, I deserve to rest. I'll make a few appropriate "grunts" to my wife and children and that'll take care of my husbandly and fatherly duties.* Would that sort of reasoning work on your job? Again, your choice gets back to what's important. Communicating is important, but it takes effort. If "closing a sale" to a client meant mustering up whatever energy you have left, I know you would do what was necessary. And again, what—or who—is more important in God's eyes, and should be in yours as well, than your dear sweet wife?

Turning a Corner

Well, my friend, I hope you squirmed a bit as we talked about living with your wife in an understanding way. I know this chapter is running a little longer than the others, but this is a most important principle for you and me as husbands to implement in our marriage. The Bible gives us as Christians an abundance of general commands to follow, but very few specific commands that are addressed specifically to us as husbands. That means we should really pay attention to those specific commands, don't you think? And brother, this is one: "Husbands...dwell with them with understanding, giving honor to the wife, as to a weaker vessel, and as being heirs together of the grace of life" (1 Peter 3:7). We do well to heed God's direction for us as husbands. So, are you ready to make some changes? Are you ready to turn a corner in your relationship with your wife? I know I've been convicted of this myself as I've been writing!

But where do you and I start? First, take a little "pop quiz" to determine your current level of communication with your companion-for-life. Check which statement best describes your attitude about connecting with your wife. Which husband are you?

- ❏ "What? Did you say something? Were you talking to me?"

- ❏ "Sure I'm listening! By the way, what's for dinner?"

- ❏ "Let's talk while we watch the football game."

- ❏ "Let me tell you what I think."

- ❏ "Take as much time as you need; I'm listening."

How well did you do? I'm sure you're probably like me and recognized that you're guilty of saying or thinking each of these statements at one time or another. I think you will agree that there is always room for improvement. So, what's next?

Make an effort to communicate. Determine to talk to your wife as soon as you get home each day or when she gets home. Have a brief agenda of questions ready to ask her—questions like, "How was your day?...Any problems at home?...How can I help you this evening?...Do the children need any help with their homework?" I'm sure you can think of other kinds of questions you can ask to enhance your communication with your wife each day.

Plan a time for communicating. Take your efforts one step further and set aside time to be alone with your wife so that *together* (and alone!) you can talk about life, the future, your mutual dreams, and your goals as a couple. Plan an evening out for just the two of you. Go to a quiet place and force yourself to communicate. Make the effort. That's right—I said *force* yourself to talk. If you're anything like me (and I know you probably are), I'll gladly let my wife come up with all the topics for discussion and then passively answer when questioned. So try taking some of the burden of communication off your wife's shoulders and take some initiative. Plan a time for communicating.

> Let's be careful with what we *don't say,* as well as make an effort to edify in what we *do say.*

Realize that communication is more than just words. Have you ever heard the saying, "Actions speak volumes"? Up to this point we've talked about verbal communication. This is where most men I've talked to have a problem. They just don't talk to their wives! But if communication expert Albert Mehrabian is correct in his research, there is also a need for us to work on our nonverbal skills as well, or our actions. This is what Mr. Mehrabian discovered:

> As much as 55 percent of a message we send may be communicated nonverbally through action. Another 38 percent of a message may be communicated through tone of voice. That leaves only 7 percent communicated through spoken words.[6]

Wow! That means that our tone of voice and how we act around our wife communicates up to 93 percent of our thoughts and feelings toward her! So let's be careful with what we *don't say*, as well as make an effort to edify in what we *do say*.

The Blessings of Good Communication

I said at the beginning of this book that my wife, Elizabeth, and I are simultaneously writing books that will complement one another—me to the husbands, and her to the wives. This has been great for our own communication, to discuss our chapters with each other so the books can help both husbands and wives work on certain key issues in their marriages. For this particular chapter we put our heads together and came up with the following list of blessings that result from better communication between husbands and wives. If you and your wife are reading this chapter together, be our guest and add to our list of blessings!

∞ God is honored when we do things His way.

∽ Your friendship with your wife is strengthened.

∽ Your marital relationship takes on greater meaning.

∽ Misunderstandings are diminished.

∽ Peace and harmony are reinforced.

∽ Teamwork is enhanced.

∽ Learning is reciprocal.

∽ Intimacy is promoted.

One author of a book for men considered communication to be a significant factor in a positive marriage. I trust you are beginning to agree and that you will determine to be a better communicator with your wife. Why? Because...

> How we communicate with our wives will produce either good or bad consequences. If we communicate poorly, it will have a negative effect on the marriage relationship. Communication is the vehicle that is used to accomplish many responsibilities and relational aspects of marriage. Without it a husband can neither lead properly, nor communicate love effectively. One can neither address issues without it, nor resolve conflict without it.[7]

Case closed! We had better learn to communicate!

Little Things That Make
a Big Difference

1. Choose to listen.

Listening is an act of love. When you listen to your wife, you are communicating nonverbally that she is an important person to you. You value her by valuing what she says. God has given you two ears—that should tell you something about the importance of listening! Your ears are your most important communication tool. Learn to listen. Then choose to listen.

2. Talk about what interests your wife.

Communication is not a one-way street. If you want your wife to listen to you and talk about what you think is important, then start talking about what is interesting and important to her. What are her interests? Make an effort to know what type of books she likes to read, her hobbies, and her gift-edness for ministry. Then take the next step and prepare yourself to talk with her about those interests. (Then you can be sure she will be all ears when you want to talk about Saturday's big game!)

3. Observe your wife's nonverbal communication.

Communication is not so much about what you say, as what you *don't* say. You need to be sensitive to your wife's mannerisms. Like you, she gets tired.

She lives with a large amount of stress. She gets behind. So to keep from saying the wrong thing or hurting her feelings in some way, look for those nonverbal hints that tell you to save some communication until later. But if it's too late and you've already blurted out the wrong thing—or the right thing at the wrong time—saying, "I'm sorry" can go a long way.

4. Think of topics to talk about.

If your wife is like most wives, then she's probably tired of being the initiator of conversations. It's time for you to come up with topics for discussions. Salesmen do this all the time before they visit a client. Why not make the same kind of effort in your own home? All it takes to communicate well is a little thought and a lot of care. On your way home from work make a mental list of issues, current events, spiritual subjects, whatever. Then you'll be ready to initiate a conversation when you get home, or when you take your wife on a date. She will be relieved to not have to work so hard at getting you to talk. Why, you may end up talking so much that she won't be able to get a word in, and she will be thrilled.

5. Mind your manners with your wife.

    ∽   Never interrupt her while she is talking to you or another person.

∽ Never belittle or put her down in front of others, especially your children. Make this your habit whether people are present or not.

∽ Never criticize or correct her in public, even as a joke. A godly husband refrains from running down another, and especially his wife (James 4:11), refrains from degrading humor (Ephesians 5:4), and refrains from sarcasm (Proverbs 26:24-25).

∽ Always compliment her in the presence of others, especially your children.

∽ Never bring up her past failures. God has forgiven your wife, and so should you.

6. Identify speech patterns that must go.

This "little thing" speaks of personal speech habits and mannerisms—*how* you say *what* you say. Do you tend to raise your voice when you communicate with your wife? Do you have an angry tone when you talk? Are you communicating like a drill sergeant?

4

Enjoying Intimacy

Several months ago I taught a workshop at a pastor's conference entitled "How to Be the Husband of a Happy Pastor's Wife." In my talk I shared a number of ways that each man could cultivate a more meaningful relationship with his wife. When I was through with my presentation, I opened up the meeting for discussion. Was I ever surprised as the majority of the questions asked were about sexual intimacy! Frankly, I was totally unprepared as the questions about sex started rolling in. I speak on and answer questions on this most personal aspect of the marriage relationship all the time, but my message to these men had nothing to do with the subject. Their line of questioning was a complete curve ball!

With the memory of that workshop in my mind, I come to this chapter in our book and can declare with confidence that intimacy in marriage is an issue that most definitely needs to be addressed! A right perspective on this area of our lives is important if we want to be a husband after God's own heart.

Created for Intimacy

How would you define intimacy? If you're like most men (including yours truly), you would probably define intimacy as sexual intercourse or lovemaking. Well, you would be at least *partially* right. God did include physical union as part of the marriage package, as we see in the Scriptures: "A man shall leave his father and mother and be joined to his wife, and they shall become one flesh" (Genesis 2:24).

But intimacy for a couple can and should be much more than merely sexual, as important as that is. At this point most men, in a state of utter puzzlement, will ask the question, "Well...what else is there besides sexual intimacy?" Again, while this is important, it's just a part of intimacy. Let's look now at some other aspects of intimacy, which all work together to make a more pleasurable marriage.

Intimacy is a close friendship. Did you have a close buddy in high school or college or do you have a longtime workmate who was or is so close to you that the two of you could talk about anything? That's the kind of intimacy you should have with your wife, because intimacy includes friendship. Maybe you already have this kind of close friendship with your sweetheart. If you do, you know that it's great, isn't it? And you probably also know that you shouldn't take it for granted, and that you should continue to nurture that closeness with your most intimate friend—your wife.

But maybe you don't have this kind of friendship-intimacy with your wife at this point in your marriage. You might have been great friends at one time, but in the busyness of life, your friendship has waned. Many marriages do go through such "dry" periods. But those dry spells don't need to last. Do you desire to regain that friend you once had in your wife (and I can't imagine why you wouldn't)? Well, there's hope! Read on and pray that one day God will develop in you the heart of a friend, that one day in the not-too-distant future your wife could say of her relationship with you, "This is my beloved, and this is my friend" (Song of Solomon 5:16).

As I'm writing this, I'm having another thought I can't resist sharing. I'm thinking that this type of friendship-intimacy is also what we should desire to have with God. We need to have such a close relationship with God through our Lord Jesus Christ that, like Abraham of old, we too are a "friend of God" (James 2:23). That, my friend, is the ultimate intimacy!

Now, back to your marriage....

Intimacy is a mood. We might even call it a feeling, an attitude, or a state of mind. The mood of intimacy usually expresses itself in a place. This place could be anywhere. It can be any place where you and your wife are able to focus your attention exclusively on the other. That place can be the breakfast table, where you and your honey share a quiet dinner after the kids are in bed; a corner booth at your favorite restaurant, where you both enjoy each other and a bottomless cup of coffee; a tree-lined street or a beach or a park where the two of you can savor a stroll at sunset.

I hope you can see why building a friendship with your wife would encourage this attitude or mood of intimacy. Personally, I'm always concerned about couples who never seem to be or want to be alone. They are constantly doing things with others. Dinners, plays, concerts, and outings, even vacations, are always enjoyed in the context of a group.

Intimacy, however, is private, privately shared, and privately developed. It is a state of mind that binds you and your wife together. It was that state of mind that promoted a desire for intimacy in the first place. Your goal is to grow to the place that, no matter where you are, your intimate friendship makes you feel as if it's just the two of you who are alone together. If you desire this brand of closeness, then you must start building or continue building a best-friendship with your wife. Then I guarantee that both you and she will constantly be thinking of each other, and eagerly awaiting your private times together!

Intimacy is understanding. How do you get to know and understand another person? By spending time with him or her. The more you know your wife as a person, know her thoughts, and know her dreams, the more intimate your understanding of her will be. Elizabeth and I have been married for a long time (now let's see...is it 37...or 38 years?). Spending that many years around another person gives you a pretty good insight into that person's inner life, and I think that I can truthfully say that's the case with Elizabeth and me. But I can also truth-fully say that over the years it's been a constant battle for us to make sure we stay connected because, like every couple, we've both been growing, maturing, and changing.

Unfortunately, that's not true about many couples. They have not attempted to stay involved in each other's lives—to continue learning about their spouse. And I know, because I've done a lot of marriage counseling through the decades as a pastor! A deeper level of intimacy may have been present at the beginning of the marriage, but slowly, over time and in the flow of the busy-ness of life, and due to uninten-tional neglect, that inti-mate communion was lost. Thirty or 40 years later the product is a marriage made up of two complete strangers living under the same roof, with very little in common. These are the couples you see in a restaurant eating their entire meal in total silence. What a sad scene! And what's even more tragic is knowing that this estrangement could have been avoided. So please, don't let life and all its distractions keep you and the love-of-your-life from continually—on a daily basis—re-acquainting yourselves with each other's growth and development. This kind of intimate understanding will definitely foster the final type of intimacy in your mar-riage—sexual intimacy.

> Every good marriage must be a friendship between two people who are willing to sacrifice for the other person.

Intimacy is a close physical relationship. We've been talking about intimacy created through the development of a deep friendship with your wife. Every good marriage must be a friendship between two people who are willing to sacrifice for the other person. You as a husband must think as much of your wife as you think of any friend. And you must have as much interest in her as any two best friends have in each other.

But marriage is more than just being good friends. Much more! Guys can be friends, and so can sisters or two women or a group of women. In every good marriage, however, the husband-and-wife friendship goes one significant step further and goes on to develop into a passionate physical union, goes on to nurture a close physical relationship that fulfills each other sexually, goes on to be a never-ending, fresh surprise to each other sexually, goes on to enjoying one another as if you were still newlyweds.

Exactly how can you keep this intimate passion burning for the life of a marriage? To repeat, it all starts with the fuel of a faithful friendship, mutual respect, and clear communication. And now, we add that it also requires a decisive commitment to stand watch over the fire of sexual intimacy—to stoke it, to rekindle it, to do whatever it takes to keep it burning...even if that means going to the mall! (I once heard a speaker say, "If you want to have sex with your wife, you have to be willing to go to the mall with her!")

Created Differently

God created man and woman in His own image, and both bear the creative workmanship of an all-powerful God

(Genesis 1:27). Also, men and women who are Christians are viewed as spiritually similar, as one in Christ Jesus (Galatians 3:28). But when it comes to anatomy and physiology, God, in His great wisdom and for His own good reasons, wired men and women differently. Part of this difference is because of the different roles men and women are to fulfill in a marriage. The man is to provide, and the woman is to nurture. The man is to give strong, protective leadership, and the woman is to support and sustain life and living.

All this to say, the many issues and problems that have their origin in our physical differences also extend to sexual intimacy. That's why my pastor friends had so many questions. Men and women think and act differently about many issues, including sex.

My personal opinion as to why sexual intimacy is such a problem for married couples is that one or both partners fails to understand, or seriously consider, or refuses to accept that there are differences. This lack of understanding leads to faulty reasoning like, *My wife should respond the same way as I do when it comes to sex.* Then when she doesn't, we wonder, *What's wrong with her?...* and...well, you know the rest. So I repeat, take the time to better understand your wife and male/female differences. It will make a big difference! I know we've looked at this verse before, but it again reminds us of what it means to be a husband after God's own heart:

> Husbands, likewise, dwell with [your wife] with understanding, giving honor to the wife, as to the weaker vessel, and as being heirs together of the grace of life (1 Peter 3:7).

As this scripture teaches us, the wife is "the weaker vessel." This points specifically to her physical abilities. Generally speaking, women have less stamina, less physical strength and energy then men. And you as the husband who desires to live with her "with understanding" need to care enough to discover how you can give honor to the differences between you and your wife. You need to learn how to live with those differences and how to love and accept every one of them. Intimacy at all levels, and especially at the physical level, begins with understanding that you and your wife are different. Then your next step is to apply the following guidelines for greater enjoyment of intimacy.

> True biblical love is a selfless commitment of one's body, soul, and spirit to the betterment of the other person.

The Makings of Intimacy

Intimacy, for a Christian couple, is not something that just happens. As we've seen, intimacy possesses multiple facets and is multi-layered. It is hard work. The Fall and our resultant sinful nature has left us flawed with fears, bitterness, and selfishness. Therefore we must seek God's help if we are to enjoy true and fulfilling intimacy in our marriages. God's kind of intimacy requires that you...

Make sure you offer your wife a biblical love. You can't change the world's thoughts about "love." To the world, love is romantic feelings, physical attraction, lust, and sex.

But for a Christian man, a husband after God's own heart, love is different. We're to show a biblical kind of love. What makes biblical love different? One marriage counselor defines biblical love in this way:

> A selfless and enduring commitment of the will to care about and benefit another person by righteous, truthful, and compassionate thoughts, words and actions.[8]

True biblical love is a selfless commitment of one's body, soul, and spirit to the betterment of the other person. It is a love with actions, not just words. And this, husband, is the kind of love we are to offer our wives. If you routinely and repeatedly demonstrate your love by the words you say and by your actions, the intimacy God intended will be forthcoming. No wife in her right mind could resist a husband who is giving this kind of love—Christ's love (Ephesians 5:25). She will freely share all with a husband whose chief goal in life is to sacrificially love her as Christ loved the church.

Make a covenant with your eyes. A *covenant* is a serious commitment a man after God's own heart makes with God. And that is what is needed if we are to keep ourselves pure for our wives. Job did just that when he said, "I have made a covenant with my eyes; why then should I look upon a young woman?" (Job 31:1).

It's no secret that men can easily become sexually stimulated simply by looking at a woman. Therefore it's important that we monitor the "eye gate." You and I are in no way planning to commit adultery with our body, but...we just might be committing adultery with our eyes. Jesus spoke about wandering, longing gazes at any woman other than your wife in Matthew 5:27 when He said, "Whoever looks at a woman to lust for her has *already committed adultery* with her in his heart." As one scholarly source explains,

> Jesus indicated that the sin [of adultery] described in Exodus 20:14 lies deeper than the overt act. "Whoever looks" characterizes the man whose glance is not checked by holy restraint, and who forms the impure purpose of lusting after her. The act will follow when opportunity occurs.[9]

Friend, realize that intimacy means mutual purity. Your wife is to be keeping herself pure for you. And God is asking you to do the same for her...and that purity starts with your eyes. So...make a covenant with your eyes!

Make your wife's body the standard. Like it or not, you and I are a product of our culture *and* of the Fall. We are affected by the sex-crazed society we live in. So much of what we see has sex connected with it. "Sex sells" is Madison Avenue's motto. As a result, we come to view the women in TV ads or the "cover girls" on the checkout-stand magazines or the nicely dressed women at the office as "the standard" for women. Then we come home to a wife who's had two preschoolers hanging on her all day long. She hasn't had one minute to herself, let alone time to change out of the sweats she was wearing when you left for work earlier that morning. Upon looking at her and seeing she doesn't measure up to our "fantasy," we can be tempted to become discontent. That's the moment we must look to God for His help in resisting the temptation to "deal treacherously with the wife of [our] youth" (Malachi 2:15).

Husband, God says that your *wife* is to be your standard! *"She* is your companion and your wife by covenant" (verse 14). Do you remember your marriage vows? They probably went something like this: "In sickness and health, for better or for worse, till death you do part." In your marriage vows, before God and to your bride, you made your wife your one and only standard. So by remembering daily and recommitting daily to those vows, you will ensure that your *wife,* not some "fantasy model," is your model. Hers is the perfect body. Hers is the only body God says is yours to enjoy. God warns and admonishes us husbands with these words:

> Drink water from your own cistern, and running water from your own well.... Let your fountain be blessed, and rejoice with the wife of your youth.... Let her breasts satisfy you at all times; and always be enraptured with her love (Proverbs 5:15,18-19).

How's Your Heart?

Right now I think we need a heart checkup, or a marriage checkup. I'm not going to ask the obvious question —"How are you doing in the Intimacy Department?"— because if you are like my pastor friends, there are issues and areas that need some work. But don't be discouraged. Your marriage is no different than mine or all the other guys you know. No marriage is all that it could be. Why? Because you and I are not all *we* could be in our spiritual growth and maturity. And that's the challenge!

Your marriage, like mine and others, is always in need of "fine tuning." People change. Marriage partners change. The family makeup changes. And the marriage must adapt to the changes that are occurring in the two people that make up that marriage. Your ability to adapt to the ages and stages of marriage will ensure that intimacy in all its glory will always be there. Ask God to open *your* heart to changes that *you* need to make in *your* life that will encourage and enhance intimacy with your wife.

Have you noticed that I haven't said anything about your wife? I would have to say that in the majority of marriages, it is the wife who is waiting and praying for greater love and sensitivity on her husband's part. Even if there are problems that only your wife can change, the fact is, God calls us to change ourselves and we are directly accountable to Him for doing what's right in the marriage relationship. Scripture never calls us to attempt to change a spouse. So, what do you say to taking a few first or further steps to showing greater love and concern?

Now, I must alert you that you may find your wife to be a bit skeptical and cautious at first! This will be the case if there have been instances of insensitivity on your part. But she will more than likely (Lord willing!) respond to your God-motivated efforts. Then the two of you can continue traveling on the road of a marriage that honors God and gives you both all of the intimacy each of you desires and can handle. Sounds great, doesn't it? It should sound great, because that's what God meant when He created man and woman to enjoy intimacy, to become "one flesh" (Genesis 2:24).

Little Things That Make a Big Difference

1. Communicate openly about sex.

As the years go by in a marriage, the "newness" of sex can start wearing off and the pressures of life can begin building up until intimacy seems to be less of a driving force. But every couple must be careful, because the need for intimacy is still very much present, as one marriage counselor's records show. He reports that time and time again husbands of all ages expressed that "sexual fulfillment" was #1 on their Top-Five list of "most basic needs."[10] Yet when their wives were asked for the same information, sex did not appear at all on their Top-Five list!

What this means is that you are going to have to talk openly to your wife about your ongoing needs in the Sexual Fulfillment Department. In many cases wives don't understand the male sex drive and conclude that their husbands are like they are when it comes to the frequency of desire for sex. So the next time you're alone together and the time is right, talk about scheduling sex into your busy lives. The talk will do both of you good!

2. Go to bed at the same time.

Sexual intimacy can become a major problem if you and your wife are operating on different schedules.

For example, your job might require that you work the evening or night shift. Whatever the case, make a concerted effort to plan with your wife to go to bed together. A little thing like going to bed at the same time can make a big difference in your sex life. Intimacy doesn't just happen. Being close physically generates feelings in both of you that wouldn't arise if one of you is still out in the family room watching television, "surfing the net," or poring over paperwork from the office. Don't purposefully sabotage your sex life with late-night diversions. Make sure you fulfill each other's sexual desires (1 Corinthians 7:3).

3. Take care of yourself.

The Bible says that "the husband does not have authority over his own body, but the wife does" (1 Corinthians 7:4). This means your body is not yours. It's the property of your wife! Therefore you are to be a good steward of your wife's real estate by keeping your body in good physical shape—not for your sake, but for hers. If you want your wife to be more sexually attracted to you, then do your part. Good grooming is a little thing, but it makes a big difference. Take a shower after a long, hard, hot day at the office or out in the truck.

Also, a little exercise goes a long way. You may get plenty of exercise on your job, but if you sit at a desk all day, you're not burning many calories. If you are a little or a lot out of shape, then join a gym or purchase a few weights and use them as often as you can. Take a walk in the mornings or evenings with your wife. You'll not only build intimacy, but by walking, you can lose about 12 pounds in a year without ever changing your diet. Losing a few pounds never hurts in the Lovemaking Department.

4. Make up quickly.

"Do not go to bed angry" is good advice for any married couple. Or, if you want it in stronger language, the Bible says, "Do not let the sun go down on your wrath" (Ephesians 4:26). Arguments seem to fester and grow foul if they are allowed to continue. Restore that wonderful relationship with your wife by saying, "I'm sorry." And just think of the intimate fun the two of you can have when you make up!

5. Schedule a getaway.

As I have repeatedly said, keeping intimacy alive in your marriage takes a lot of work—but it's worth it to enjoy this blessing God has provided! One of the best ways to keep the fires of passion burning in both of you is to get away on a regular basis. If you want your wife to respond to you physically, then take the initiative. Find a place that's not too far away and not too expensive. (You'll want to do this again, so don't break the bank the first time.) Find a babysitter or arrange with friends to exchange babysitting responsibilities. Getting your wife away from the distractions of the house, children, and a myriad of other things, even for an overnighter, allows for a focused time together. A getaway will rejuvenate your sex life and enhance your marriage.

5

Managing Your Money

Moreover it is required in stewards
that one be found faithful.
1 CORINTHIANS 4:1-2

My dad was a terrific father in many ways, carefully teaching me about life and living. And every day I am particularly grateful that he tutored me well in the area of money management, especially when it came to thrift. From as far back as I can remember, my father repeatedly presented me with a proposition: "Whatever you put into a savings account, I will match."

Even to a kid receiving an allowance of 25 cents a week, this sounded like a good deal. So, week after week, year after year, I faithfully saw my wise father match my meager savings. Keeping his end of the bargain never cost him very much, but his wisdom taught me one of life's valuable habits—that of thrift. This habit is so ingrained in me that even today, I can't help but apply it to everything in life that involves money (which doesn't leave out much!).

This story about my dad brings you and me as husbands after God's own heart to our next essential role in a marriage relationship—being a wise manager of money.

If you were to ask most marriage counselors what is one of the top, if not *the* top, causes of conflicts in a marriage, I believe the majority would say it's *money*—how it is acquired, how it is spent, and by whom. That's why as husbands we need to make sure we are giving strong leadership in our marriage in the area of money management. This also means that we may need to exercise a little more self-control when it comes to handling money ourselves. So it's important to understand what the Bible says about money and the management of money in order to serve as examples of wise stewardship to our wife and family.

Money Matters with God

Would you believe that the topic of money comes up more frequently than many other topics in God's Word? Obviously money and its use and our attitudes about money matters to God. Now the question is, Does it matter to you? Well-known evangelist Billy Graham believes our attitude about money is critical. He proposes:

> If a person gets his attitude toward money straight, it will help straighten out almost every other area in his life.[11]

Yes, you read it right. Having a correct biblical attitude and understanding about money and its use will positively affect many or most of the other areas of your life—including your marriage. So let's look now at this important topic and try to grasp some of God's perspective on money and its management.

Money Management Is a Spiritual Issue

I've heard it said that you can tell the spiritual maturity of a man by looking at his checkbook or his credit card statements. Well, how do yours look? What do they reveal about you...and your spiritual maturity? What would another person see if they were allowed a peek at your checkbook? Would they see checks written to missionaries, to your church, to charities? Checks written to cover the necessities of life, the needs of your family, your children's education? Or would they be staring at a long log of checks written for indulgences, excesses, frivolities, fun... you know, toys?

Money Management Is a Stewardship Issue

Whose money is it in the first place? We must understand that everything we possess—our money, our possessions, our family, everything!—is a gift from God and is on loan from Him to us. The psalmist said, "The earth is the LORD's, and all its fullness, the world and those who dwell therein" (Psalm 24:1).

So what then is our role? If God is the owner and we are the users, then we are *stewards* of God's gifts to us. And the apostle Paul said, "It is required in stewards that one be found faithful" (1 Corinthians 4:2). Friend, how faithful are you as a steward of all that God has entrusted to your safekeeping? How well do you manage and care for your wife? Your children? Your time? Your talents? Your physical body? Your spiritual gifts? And (the topic of discussion in this chapter) the making and spending of your money? God has blessed you with all of the above! Now, rate your faithful management of His blessings.

Money Management Is a Contentment Issue

Contentment is a difficult issue in our society. The television ad says, "You need this new car." The newspaper has a full-page advertisement for a family cruise or vacation to Disneyland. Wouldn't that be fun for the whole family? What a great time we could have bonding as a family, drawing closer together, etc., etc. The only problem is...what if you don't have the money? Then you would have to go into debt in order to fulfill this dream-vacation for you and your family.

> Contentment is a significant key not only to good money management, but also to the spiritual health and well-being of your family.

If you don't have money, you do have other options. For instance, maybe this year you can take your family to a favorite camping spot. Or you could stay at home and take local "mini trips" each day. In other words, be content with living within your means. Contentment is a key element in managing your money.

Can you remember a time when it was extremely hard to manage your money because there was more month than money? Every penny...and then some(!), was spoken for. Perhaps that's still true for you now. I know I have a few of those memories, especially when Elizabeth and I were first married and in college and living on $200 a month. Those were tough times for us.

Perhaps the tough times are behind you and your family. But if they're not, it may be because of a lack of contentment. Our sinful nature fights against contentment and is prone to the "wants" of life. The apostle Paul reported that he had to *learn* contentment (Philippians 4:11), and we should as well. If you don't learn the lesson of contentment, it will be very hard to manage your money well.

Learning to be content with what God gives you as a family will provide great freedom for you as the provider and for your wife as the co-manager. And, as a bonus, your children, as impressionable observers, will see the fallacy of society's delusion that wealth and possessions are a means of happiness. Contentment, then, is a significant key to not only good money management, but also to the spiritual health and well-being of your family.

Money Management Is a Giving Issue

God doesn't want or need your money. Why? Because the Bible says that God owns all the cattle on a thousand hills (Psalm 50:10)! But what God does desire is an attitude of selflessness and selfless giving. When it comes to giving, "God loves a cheerful giver" (2 Corinthians 9:7). God loves and blesses the one who gives out of a heart of love, not out of the size of his bank account. J. Oswald Sanders, famed missionary statesman, put it this way:

The basic question is not how much of our money we should give to God, but how much of God's money we should keep for ourselves.[12]

So money management—the managing of *God's* money—should start with following God's guidelines for giving. This concept of freewill giving can best be summed up by looking at the example of a group of Christians who lived in an area called Macedonia (now part of modern-day Greece). These saints were poor and afflicted, but they were rich in love and obedience. They gave selflessly and generously to God for the needs of others (2 Corinthians 8:1-6). From their hearts we learn how we should approach giving.

1. *Giving is to be appropriate.* The Macedonian Christians gave "according to their ability" (2 Corinthians 8:3). God affixes no percentages or amounts to what we give. However, He does expect us to give *according to* how we have prospered, *according to* our earnings (1 Corinthians 16:2). This was a very difficult concept to implement in my marriage when Elizabeth and I became a Christian couple. I had a good-paying job, and we had enough money to buy lots of toys such as a camper, a motorcycle, and so on. We had prospered, but we were spending every penny on ourselves! How were we to give appropriately?

I realized we had to begin choosing whether to give money to God or to continue to use that money on our own pleasures. It was a new struggle, but with God's help I chose to start giving back to God. We stopped eating out so much. We stopped traveling so much. We gave up worldly things in order to give as God had prospered us. It was a painful learning experience, because, as you know, you can easily get used to the excesses of "the good life"!

Now, let me quickly say two things. First, I'm not trying to set myself up as the standard. No, God has set the standard through the example of the dear Macedonian Christians. It is your and my privilege and joy to follow that standard. And second, it would take another entire book to even begin to share with you the many spiritual blessings our family has received as we have given of our God-given resources! My mother had always told me, "It's impossible to out-give God," and I have seen this to be true!

2. *Giving is to be sacrificial.* The poor Macedonians gave "*according* to their ability" (2 Corinthians 8:3). They gave appropriately. But they also gave "*beyond* their ability" (verse 3), teaching us that our "acceptable sacrifice" is "well pleasing to God" (Philippians 4:18). Again, for me and Elizabeth, giving started out as a sacrifice. Why? Because we initially started out with a budget that looked like this: Jim and Elizabeth 100 percent; God 0 percent. As you can see, our pleasure-seeking lifestyle had left nothing budgeted for God.

Maybe it's different for you...and I hope so! Maybe you are already giving to the Lord's work. If so, I commend you for your faithful obedience. But maybe you need to prayerfully consider giving more. Giving is a part of our worship to God, and giving *sacrificially* is an *essential* part of that worship. Has God blessed your life? I know He has, and so do you. Then why not show your love and appreciation by giving even more sacrificially? You cannot out-give God.

3. *Giving is to be voluntary.* Christianity is an amazing religion. Salvation is freely offered to us through the grace of God and cannot be earned (Ephesians 2:8-9). We also cannot buy our salvation because it has already been bought for us through the death of Jesus (Ephesians 1:7). Therefore, like the Macedonians, we are to be "freely willing" in our giving (2 Corinthians 8:3). We are to give voluntarily because we want to give. We are to give willingly out of a heart that is overflowing with love for and gratitude to our Savior, the Lord Jesus Christ.

As I'm sure you can see, the wise management of your money is a vital discipline for you and me as husbands. Why? I repeat, because the way you manage God's money—the way it is spent and how it is given—is an indicator of your spiritual maturity. And the level of *your* spiritual maturity will critically affect the spiritual maturity of your wife and children. Now that we've reaffirmed this, let's look at a few reasons why money and its management should matter in your marriage.

Money Matters in Marriage

If Dr. Billy Graham is correct about the importance of having a right attitude toward money, then it's also true that our attitude toward money can have a pivotal effect on our marriage. Unfortunately, the world and our own sinful nature often produces some rather wrong attitudes when it comes to money. These attitudes are what often create tension and conflict in a marriage. For instance:

Covetousness—means to have a strong desire to possess something that belongs to someone else. The Bible says that your conduct should be "without covetousness" and that you should "be content with such things as you have" (Hebrews 13:5). (There's contentment again!) If you and I are content with what we have, we will not be discontent with what we don't have.

Take your neighbor Joe's new boat, for example. You shouldn't want his boat. Why? First, because it is sin to covet someone else's property. And second, buying a boat might not be good money management on your part. I live in the state of Washington, and the standing joke is that the two happiest days in a man's life are #1—the day he buys his boat, and #2—the day he sells it. And what happens in between day 1 and day 2? Another Washingtonian saying goes into effect: Owning a boat is like shoveling your money into a black hole!

All this to say, don't covet Joe's boat! And remember, God's cure for covetousness is contentment.

Idolatry—is putting someone or something else ahead of God. When you trust in money rather than or more than you trust in God, you are committing idolatry. Paul warned those who were rich not to "trust in uncertain riches but in the living God" (1 Timothy 6:17). Therefore a man after God's own heart trusts in God. Why? Because God is the one "who gives us richly all things to enjoy" (verse 17). Money is a false god and, as the apostle Paul said, the "love of money is a root of all kinds of evil" (verse 10). Asking yourself these questions will surface any hint of idolatry in your attitude about money:

   ∽   Do you think and worry about money frequently?

- ✍ Do you give up family priorities to make more money?

- ✍ Do you spend a large amount of your time caring for your things?

- ✍ Is it hard for you to give money for the Lord's work?

Brother, loving money can do nothing for you. And loving money will surely affect your relationship with God. Jesus said, "No one can serve two masters; for either he will hate the one and love the other, or else he will be loyal to the one and despise the other. You cannot serve God and mammon [riches]" (Matthew 6:24). Serving money can only harm you and your loved ones. So whether you have resources or not, don't lust for money or for more of it. Work hard for your means, and trust God to provide for the needs of your family. Put your faith and trust in the one person who can help you in this world and also in the next—the Lord Jesus Christ.

Worldliness—is akin to materialism, and goes a step further to become an overly flirtatious desire for possessions and pleasure. We as Christians are in this world but we are not to be consumed with the things of this world (1 John 2:15). That's worldliness. We are merely sojourners and pilgrims who are passing through

> Managing money wisely matters to God...and it should matter to you.

this world (1 Peter 2:11). We are citizens of heaven (Philippians 3:20), and we are to be eagerly awaiting the return of our King. When it comes to worldliness, you and I can easily recognize when we've become worldly because along with worldliness usually comes a trail of debt! But in our worldliness, we don't always recognize debt's danger signals. Check these danger signals and see if any apply to your family's financial condition.

- A large share—20 percent or more—of your take-home pay goes toward debt payments.

- Your debt payments are being stretched over longer periods of time.

- You are adding new debt before paying off old ones.

- You are paying off debt with debt.

- You are often delinquent on payments.

One sure solution to worldliness is to follow the apostle Paul's admonition to "set your mind on things above, not on things on the earth" (Colossians 3:2). This one piece of advice will set us in the right direction, away from the lures of worldliness.

By now I'm guessing you can see why money is such a "hot button" for couples. You and your wife came into your marriage with certain habits and disciplines concerning money that must now become *God's* habits and disciplines—the kind we've been addressing in this chapter. So please, determine that you will not be a husband who has a covetous eye, an idolatrous spirit, or a worldly attitude. As a husband after God's own heart, you need to take an active role in leading your wife and family in the area of financial responsibility. Managing money wisely matters to God…and it should matter to you.

Money Management Should Matter to You

So far we've considered some pretty serious truths and facts about money. Having a proper attitude toward money and exercising diligence in managing it is a great responsibility that you and I must shoulder as husbands. Money management is not our wife's responsibility. Oh, she may help with the management and bill-paying. But money management is a function of leadership—our leadership as husbands. Therefore you and I as men and husbands need to step up to the plate when it comes to the finances of our home. It's not enough to just *make* the money. We must also actively *manage* it.

Those of us who are "managers" at whatever level in whatever enterprise know that managing isn't always a one-person arrangement. We know we don't always need to personally do it ourselves. We can delegate some of the work to others. Well, that same principle applies to managing the household budget. You and I don't always have to be the only one involved with the family's money.

Here's how I've applied this principle in my marriage over the years. As long as there was enough money in our family bank accounts for my wife Elizabeth to pay the bills without getting an ulcer from having to decide who would get paid and who would have to wait, I welcomed her assistance with the bookkeeping and bill-paying. But during those "hard times" earlier in our marriage, the lean times when such agonizing decisions had to be made, then as the leader I made those decisions. As I said, this has been my approach. You might have a different one, and that's okay. The point is, my wife and I work together as a team to manage the family finances. And hopefully you and your wife are doing the same.

Now, I must make one last comment before we move on. I know there are men who just don't want to bother with money matters, so they "delegate" that responsibility to their wife. Other husbands rationalize that because their wife is better with numbers and figures, they may as well entrust the whole sphere of financial management to her. Christian man, whether you want to or not, or whether your wife is better at finances or record-keeping or not, don't abdicate your role as a L-E-A-D-E-R in the area of money management. Take on a greater leadership role in your family finances. How?

- Look to those who can give you wise financial counsel

- Embrace your leadership role in money management

- Attend seminars or courses on family finances

- Determine to grow wise in your money management

- Establish the roles you and your wife play in money matters

- Read books on money management

The Windows of Heaven

Husband, I hope you understand by now the importance of faithfulness in the area of money management. Yes, it takes work, but consider just a few of the many blessings that will be yours! Being a faithful steward of God's money will result in *God* being glorified. Your *wife* will be blessed as you model self-control when it comes to the stuff of this world. Your *children* will be blessed and influenced by your financial leadership (just as my dad's leadership impacted me). And *you* will be blessed by your obedience. And as a result of your obedience and stewardship, there will be the added blessing of seeing God, who has blessed you, use His money to bless *others* through your generous giving.

Talk about "compounded interest"! You'll experience "compounded blessings" as you are obedient to the Lord in just this one area of your life and marriage! God challenges you and me with this invitation:

> "Try Me now in this," says the LORD of hosts, "if I will not open for you the windows of heaven and pour out for you such blessing that there will not be room enough to receive it" (Malachi 3:10).

Man, oh man! Now *this* is what I want to be a part of! How about you?

Little Things That Make a Big Difference

1. Give to God first.

In the Old Testament, God's people were commanded to offer the first portion of their crops to God as a tribute to His abundant provision. In the New Testament, too, we are to give according to how we "prosper" (1 Corinthians 16:2). But the principle of "giving off the top"—the firstfruits—is a good way you and your wife can acknowledge your trust in God's provision for you and your family, not only today but also for the future. (And, considering the weakness and selfishness of mankind, there probably won't be anything left to give God from the "bottom"!) So give to God first. Then trust that "God is able to make all grace abound toward you, that you, always having all sufficiency in all things, may have an abundance for every good work" (2 Corinthians 9:8).

2. Have a budget.

Most financial experts say the starting point for money management is having a budget. Without a budget, you and your wife will probably buy things that are not essential. A plan for saving and spending gives the two of you boundaries and defines what's important. Just purchase a standard "Household Budget" workbook and start following the directions. But the real key to a budget is making it together with your wife and being in agreement as to what's in and what's not in your budget. Then you can hold each other accountable and celebrate and enjoy the benefits that having— and sticking to—a budget brings your way.

3. Pray over major purchases.

Since the money you are to manage is really God's money, shouldn't He be consulted as to how you spend it? Hopefully you and your wife have already committed your budget to the Lord. The two of you have prayed about what should be included in your monetary plan. Therefore, if something is in the budget, you don't necessarily need to pray about it again (although that's a good practice). So this point of praying over major purchases has to do with nonbudgeted purchases. You and your wife will want to pray for answers to questions like, How will this purchase impact our budget? Can the purchase of a newer car be delayed by fixing the "clunker" just one more time? These are the kinds of prayers and questions that are necessary when making decisions about major purchases.

4. Get organized.

Finances are complicated, even with the simplest of incomes. You and your wife should institute a financial filing system to keep track of important documents and financial statements. So purchase an accordion file folder with slots for each month of the year. Then drop your bills into the month they are due. As the bills are paid, drop in the receipts. At the end of the year you have everything handy in one place that you need for tax purposes.

5. Declare a "day of fasting" from spending money.

In Bible times, fasting usually applied to food and was a religious exercise. Because those who fasted were not eating, their interests were diverted from the physical realm to the spiritual life. Similarly, when you implement a money-fast, you allow your interests to be turned from the "stuff" of life to the "staff of life." And, as an added benefit, you and your wife come one day closer to staying within your budget. Now, that's a praise! So take calendar in hand, pick a day, and proclaim it "a day of fasting."

6. Make a list of ways to cut expenses.

You and your wife should realize that your finances are a reflection of your spiritual condition. Isn't self-control a fruit of the Spirit (Galatians 5:23)? And aren't you a steward of God's money? Whether you have enough money or not, cutting expenses will do you good. If you don't have enough money, trimming your costs will give you back some of what you need. To get started, take your new budget in hand and together see what you and your wife can lop off and live without. If you have a sufficiency of money, cutting expenses to give more to God will help you and your wife to "set your mind on things above, not on things on the earth" (Colossians 3:2).

6

Keeping Up the Home

*Through wisdom a house is built,
and by understanding it is established;
by knowledge the rooms are filled
with all precious and pleasant riches.*
PROVERBS 24:3-4

Almost 30 years ago I made my first visit to the vast country of India, a visit that marked my life forever. Since then I have taken at least 15 additional trips to India, and I have to report that India is a land of great spiritual darkness and oppression. My impression is it seems that Satan has concentrated much of his evil and tyranny on this land, making it a difficult place to minister.

While on one of my treks in India, I heard about a remarkable village. This village and its people were not unlike the thousands of other villages and people in the country. The people were poor and lived in deplorable conditions. But God had chosen this town and its people as a trophy for Himself, and the villagers had come to Christ almost en masse. God had transformed their souls and, as a result, the people began to transform their settlement and its homes into a thing of beauty.

And the result? In the midst of a land of satanic oppression and brutal poverty, this village became a beautiful and joyous testimony of the reality of Christ, like "a city that is set on a hill and cannot be hidden" because its people are "the light of the world" (Matthew 5:14). The difference between Christianity and Hinduism was very much evidenced by the way this colony of believers in Christ presented itself visually to the watching world.

As I heard this story while sitting on the hard bench of a train rattling across India, my thoughts took me back to my home in America. I wondered, *Is the difference between my religion and the religion (or lack of religion!) of my neighbors first evidenced in the way my home presents itself to their watching eyes? Do I take enough care and pride in my home and in the people who live in my home to the point that others would see it and its inhabitants as a shining witness and sparkling testimony of what I believe?*

Needless to say, I returned home with a new outlook and perspective on my home and what it should represent.

God's Perspective on the Home

Yes, I had a "wake-up call" those many years ago in the area of keeping up the home. The story of that village really started me thinking about the care of my own home. If you're a husband who desires to understand the importance of your home as a place of refuge and as a place of witness, then read on. This chapter adds to our growing list of essentials that a husband after God's own heart must consider and implement into his marriage. Let's look first at our home from God's perspective.

A home is built by wisdom—Wisdom is defined as the application of knowledge. And, at times, wisdom is just plain ol' common sense. But in whatever way it comes, you and I desperately need wisdom if we are to be the husbands God desires us to be. There are a multitude of decisions we need to make when we lead a family. And, brother, every one of those decisions must be made with wisdom! As Proverbs states, "Through wisdom a house is built, and by understanding it is established. By knowledge the rooms are filled with all precious and pleasant riches" (Proverbs 24:3-4).

> There is no greater treasure than a husband...who models godliness before his wife and children on a daily basis.

Our immediate response to this God-inspired truth should be "Sign me up! Where do I get this wisdom?" And the first obvious answer is *from the Bible,* the ultimate source of wisdom. In the Bible we find "all things that pertain to life and godliness" (2 Peter 1:3). We also gain wisdom *from prayer.* The apostle James wrote, "If any of you lacks wisdom, let him ask of God, who gives to all liberally and without reproach, and it will be given to him" (James 1:5). We can also receive wisdom *from our spouse.* God has given us wives to assist in making decisions. It's the "two are better than one" biblical axiom of marriage

(Ecclesiastes 4:9). Plus we can acquire wisdom *from wise men*. God has given you and me wise men at the church to consult when it comes to running our homes. Let's be wise husbands and take advantage of the "multitude of counselors" God has provided (Proverbs 24:6).

A home is built by godliness—"Godliness refers to having the proper attitude and conduct before God in everything."[13] Don't you think this kind of godly conduct around your house would honor God? And don't you think God would bless you for modeling this kind of conduct? Again, in the book of Proverbs, we learn that "in the house of the righteous there is much treasure" (15:6). There is no greater treasure than a husband and father who is desirous of having his be a "house of the righteous" and who models godliness before his wife and children on a daily basis.

But there is also the opposite possibility as Proverbs 15:6 goes on to say—"in the revenue of the wicked is trouble." Friend, neither of us wants trouble, so let's choose to lead our homes in a godly manner. The choice is ours—treasure or trouble? Which will yours be? Will you choose God's way and pursue righteousness?

A home is built by leadership—As a young husband I was continually told, "Your home is the proving ground for your leadership in the church." The Bible backs this up with a statement regarding the qualifications for a leader in the church: "If a man does not know how to rule his own house, how will he take care of the church of God?" (1 Timothy 3:5).

Whether you aspire to leadership in your church or not, God is still asking that you lead in your home. From the very day God created man, He designed the man to lead his family. Think about this: When you do not fulfill your role as the leader in your home, you are functioning outside the will of God. And I think you will agree with me...that's not a good thing for you or your family! If you are not where you need to be in this vital responsibility of leading in your home, ask God for His help. And seek out the help of other men who can disciple you in this all-important area of providing leadership in your home. Determine to be more obedient to God's plan for you to be the leader of your home.

A home is built by care—So far I've been talking about the *spiritual* care you and I as godly husbands are to give to our homes and our families. Friend, this must be the starting point! Our spiritual character is the foundation stone for a home that is built on wisdom and will honor God and leave a legacy of godliness. And there is one additional responsibility that I believe God asks of us as husbands, and that is the *physical* care of our house, home, or apartment. We are to diligently keep our homes in good physical condition (see Proverbs 24:3).

Picture someone walking along a road and observing a vineyard and seeing this sight: It was "all overgrown with thorns; its surface was covered with nettles; its stone wall was broken down" (Proverbs 24:31). What was the writer's evaluation of the owner? He was a "lazy man...devoid of understanding" (verse 30). Brother, just as that vineyard was a reflection of its owner, your home is a reflection of who you are as a person...

...which takes me back to my story about that little village in India. The villagers showed their *spiritual* transformation by *physically* transforming their homes into simple places of cleanliness, care, and beauty. Those townspeople didn't have much money, but they did what they could, and the difference was clearly evident. And we don't need a lot of money either. I'm not talking about spending large amounts of money on your place or having the most expensive house on your block. No, what I'm talking about is spending large amounts of time and effort to keep your home looking nice and in good working order.

Do you want your neighbors to speak well of you and your God? Then take 30 minutes and go mow the lawn. Do you want your son growing up with an appreciation for a home and its upkeep? Then allow him to assist you as you work around the house. (His wife in years to come will rise up and call you blessed!)

There is more—*much* more—that I could say about God's perspective on the home and all that it represents. But hopefully what I've shared will become a good launching pad for you to take action and do what's necessary to keep up your house. That's what a husband after God's heart does!

The Husband's Role at Home

I often accompany my wife to her women's seminars. Needless to say, I have many opportunities throughout these events to speak to the ladies and listen as they pour out their hearts about their desires to be godly wives and mothers. But many times they express that they have one huge problem—a husband back home who isn't doing his part to shoulder the burden of the home and its management. In many cases these poor women feel there is more that could—and should—be done by their husbands to help out around the home.

After listening to these wives and the struggles they describe, I've come to see there are several categories of husbands. As you read through the following list, see if you recognize yourself. See, too, how you can make sure you're doing your part around the house.

Workaholic—This is a husband who works *a lot!* Either by choice or because of the requirements of his job, he is working more than the usual 40 hours per week. In fact, he even brings some of his work home every night. Then there is the one-hour commute each way to work. This man leaves while it's still dark, and he gets home after dark. So, when does he mow the lawn, take out the trash, and do the other maintenance jobs around the house? These are valid questions.

If this scenario describes you, then alternative solutions need to be found for keeping up your home. For instance, perhaps you can hire a gardener. Hire a handyman. Hire a pool man. If there are older children, maybe you should train them to help around the house. Another option is for your wife to agree to do some of the yard work, clean the pool, or take care of other tasks in return for the money that these services would have cost. This then becomes her "Proverbs 31 Project." (If you're not sure what this means, ask your wife. She'll know about Proverbs 31!)

Finally, there is always Saturday. I know you're tired. You've put in a long week already. But God's kind of husband *gives up* some of his favorite Saturday activities...or rest, and forces himself to get out there and do some of those routine but necessary projects as well as those that have been on hold for months. Your wife will love you for it, and she will be relieved that she doesn't have to nag you anymore! What can you *give up* to make this happen?

Peter Pan—We all know the story of Peter Pan. He was a perpetual child. He had no responsibilities and he wanted none. Unfortunately, there are a lot of husbands like that today. They have their "toys" that they play with every night after work and on the weekends, so there isn't time to do the work around the house. The Peter Pan-type husband is often a sportsman. Golf, fishing, softball...just name it and he plays it! Again, this describes many husbands. For them, any excuse is valid as long as it keeps him from assuming responsibility for keeping up the home!

What happens when a husband is a Peter Pan-type? Since her husband won't take charge, the wife ends up treating him like one of the children. She's the woman who says, "I have four children, including my husband." Friend, when you married, you vowed to lead and provide for your wife and to take care of her and your home. These are obligations that come with marriage. If you're a Peter Pan husband, it's time to *grow up* and take on the responsibility of keeping up the home.

Mr. Couch Potato—Do you remember the lazy man and his vineyard in Proverbs 24? That's Mr. Couch Potato. He has the time to keep the house up, but he's too lazy or feels too tired to do it. Listen to this description of such a husband's activity around the house: "As a door turns on its hinges, so does the lazy man on his bed. The lazy man buries his hand in the bowl; it wearies him to bring it back to his mouth" (Proverbs 26:14-15). Pretty pathetic, isn't it?

Now I do want to give Mr. Couch Potato a little slack. He does have a job. He does work hard at his job. He does "provide." But therein lies his problem. He is among those under the widespread delusion that a husband's duties are fulfilled by having a job and bringing home a paycheck.

My friend, when you and I come home from work, that's when the *real* work—the work that will last for eternity—begins. It takes work to be a loving and conscientious husband. It takes work to show your wife you love her, not just in the words you say, but also in the acts you perform around the house. This has been a hard lesson for me, a reformed couch potato, to learn. Let me explain.

Most wives receive their greatest joy and fulfillment from their home. "Home" represents security, peace, and a sense of belonging. That's why your wife is always fussing with the house, moving the furniture, fixing things up. That's also why, when something is wrong and she can't fix it, like a leaking roof, or a dripping faucet, or an overgrown lawn, her nature becomes unsettled. She needs her "nest" made right. She needs it fixed! So, if you are a couch potato, set your personal wants aside, show your wife you love her, and take the initiative when it comes to fulfilling your part of keeping up the home. *Get up* off the couch and fix it or have it fixed...whatever "it" is!

Absent-minded Professor—Believe it or not, there are still some of these mentally absorbed types left roaming the planet. This husband gets preoccupied with something—anything!—and forgets all else. He's not the workaholic with his briefcase in hand. He's not a Peter Pan with his toys. He's not a couch potato with his La-Z-Boy chair in the recline position. No, he simply becomes lost in his reading, studying, working on hobbies, dabbling on his computer, or "researching" critical issues of our day on the Internet.

Oh, this husband is at home! And he's busy! But he's busy with the wrong priorities. He's doing the wrong things. Yes, reading is important, but not at the expense of keeping up the house. God's solution for such a man and husband is to be like the ant. To this man God says, "Go to the ant, you sluggard! Consider her ways and be wise...[she] provides her supplies in the summer, and gathers her food in the harvest" (Proverbs 6:6,8).

Remember what I said earlier about the "wake-up call" I received after hearing about those villagers in India? Well, I was the absent-minded professor. I was spending my nights and weekends at home studying. My roof was falling in. The yard was overgrown. On and on the list of neglect went...not to mention the neglect of my family.

So, if you are the absent-minded-professor type of husband as I was, you need to become more like the ant. You need to take care of your God-given priorities first. Then, with whatever discretionary time is left, you can "surf the Net," or do the study required to teach your men's Bible study, or enjoy your hobbies. *Wake up* as I did and realize that your first responsibility is to your family and the upkeep of your home.

Workaholic, Peter Pan, couch potato, absent-minded professor—we've looked at four kinds of husbands. You will probably admit that at one time or another, you too have acted like one or more of these kinds of husbands. You may have had times during which you've worked incessantly at your job. You may have had times when you've acted irresponsibly. You may have had times when you've functioned minimally. And last but not least, you may have had times when you've lived selfishly. Hopefully by now you are recognizing your responsibilities as the leader of your homestead and are more committed to turning some things around.

Committing to Your Home

Let me go back one last time to my story of the village in India. As I said, hearing of these noble villagers was a turning point in my commitment to my home. I was busy serving God at church and around the world as I traveled and taught God's Word at home and abroad. Obviously this was very important. All of this activity was my ministry, which was also my calling, my job, my career, my profession. But the lives of these faithful, diligent villagers forced me to stare the hard fact in the face—I was neglecting my home and the people who lived in that home. I was busy giving my testimony "out there" but was losing my testimony to my own family and in my neighborhood.

Friend, I couldn't wait to get home and begin to work on it and work on my relationships in that home. I realized that the two go hand in hand. I'm not real handy, but what a joy it was to rekindle my love for my home and its upkeep. And there was even greater joy in seeing my family respond to my attention.

> Your positive impact on the generations to come will be directly related to the ministry you have in that little place called home.

Well, that's my story. Now...what's yours? How is your commitment to *your* home and the people who live in it? Your positive impact on the generations to come will be directly related to the ministry you have in that little place called home.

The Blessing of Your Home

When was the last time you stopped to thank the Lord for the blessing of your home and the people in your home? Please, don't ever take your home for granted! Love your home. Care for your home. Praise God for your home. Maybe you and I need to take a page out of King David's life. Hear now David's heart of humble praise as he thanked God for his "house" and everything that it represented— his family and where they lived.

> Who am I, O Lord God? And what is my house, that You have brought me this far?...Therefore You are great, O Lord God. For there is none like You, nor is there any God besides You (2 Samuel 7:18,22).

Dear husband, does David's prayer and attitude reflect your heart? Can you humbly say, "Who am I, O Lord God? And what is my house, that You have brought me this far?" God has blessed your house. He has given you a wonderful family. Thank Him for them.

And if God has blessed you with a home, you must remember that all things, including the dwelling you call home, is part of your stewardship. If you want to be a better steward, maybe it's time for you and your wife to sit down together for a nice long talk about your home. Ask her what she would like to see happen around the house both spiritually and physically. What repairs will transform your place into a greater testimony of your faith? What can you budget for present needs? What can you begin to save on a weekly or monthly basis for future needs? What classes on home-improvement skills can you take at the local college or at your local home-improvement store?

One of your goals as a husband after God's own heart is to keep up your house. How can you make your home a better place for you and your wife to live? A better place to raise your children? A little bit of heaven on earth?

Little Things That Make a Big Difference

1. Ask your wife for a "to-do" list.

One of the best ways to show your wife that you love her is to help keep her "nest" in good working order. Ask your wife for a list of things around the house that need repairing. She will be very grateful. But a word of caution: If she gives you a list, make sure you work on the list. If you don't, your wife may become frustrated when you do nothing.

2. Have your own "to-do" list.

Your wife's list of things for you to do will probably be different from your list. Hers will request that you stop the dripping faucet or fix the squeaking door. But your list should include the more major repairs like the roof or furnace. If at all possible, within the boundaries of your budget, keep up the minor as well as the major repairs on your house. Deferred maintenance is always more costly than fixing a problem as it surfaces. If the money for the repair is not there, start praying for God to provide. And if your church is like most, the men are usually quick to volunteer to help with a needed repair if you let it be known.

3. Have a home-safety checklist.

     ✎   Keep chemicals and medicines locked up.

     ✎   Keep firearms doubly locked up.

- Have a fire extinguisher.
- Have a disaster plan.
- Have an exit plan in case of a fire or disaster.
- Rehearse your exit plan with the family.
- Have and check smoke detectors on a monthly basis.

4. Mow the lawn.

I should make this broader and say take care of your yard. But your lawn is the most noticeable aspect of your yard. You can have everything working nicely on the inside of the house, but if the lawn isn't mowed, people notice, including (and especially) your wife, and your house won't look good. Your wife works very hard in her domain to make the inside of the house clean and inviting. And she would like you to do the same with your domain—the yard, the outside of the house.

Yes, I know you are tired when you get home. And I know all about your favorite sports teams who play on Saturdays. But you need to mow and maintain your yard on a regular schedule. Plan a time each week and when it draws near, "psyche" yourself up to get out there in the fresh air and work in the yard. Your wife will love you for it and the neighbors will appreciate your efforts as well. (Now, for you "cliff dwellers," I say be thankful you don't have a yard to take care of. This gives you more time for that "to-do" list that your wife has for you!)

5. Clean out the garage.

When was the last time you cleaned out your garage or storage shed? It's surprising how much stuff you can amass in such a short time. Maybe you can sell off some items by getting together with your neighbors who also have things to sell and have a garage sale. Or maybe you have enough stuff of your own that you don't need additional items from your neighbors for the sale. Or maybe your church has an annual rummage sale for worthy mission projects. That annual sale can give you an annual excuse to clean out the garage. Whatever motivation you need, take it and clean out the garage. You might even have room for the car when you're done!

6. Give the gift of your time and energy.

I've got a great idea for you: On your next anniversary or special day, seize the opportunity to offer your services as a gift to your wife to fix anything around the house. A bouquet of flowers may last a week, but the gift of your hands and your time will last for years. She may have been giving a few hints about something that's been an irritating nuisance for weeks. So find a box, enclose the tools or the part that is needed for you to complete her project, and then gift-wrap the box and give it to her along with a note or certificate promising to do the job. And then DO IT! (And you'll probably still want to give the bouquet of roses, too.)

7

Raising Your Children

*And these words, which I am commanding you
today, shall be in your heart.
You shall teach them diligently to your children.*
DEUTERONOMY 6:6-7

I recently heard a man in the ministry testify to the powerful influence his father had on his life. He shared that his dad spent a great deal of time teaching him how to be a person of godly character. He then explained how this happened: The father made it a policy to spend an hour every evening after dinner with this man and his sister when they were children. Sometimes the hour was used for teaching. Other times it was spent reading with them from the Bible and other books. Then as the children grew older, the father added going over the newspaper with his son and daughter, interpreting current events in light of biblical truth. These one-hour-a-day sessions lasted until the son left home to attend college. No wonder the son was so willing to rise up and call his father blessed!

Fellow husband, it's time to add yet another element to our growing list of critical "things that really matter in your marriage"—that of parenting. At this point I am assuming you have children. If you don't, you'll still find this chapter beneficial for sharing with others who do have children, and for preparing you for the time when you and your wife have children (Lord willing). Then again, you may be a father whose children don't live in your home. If so, the basics I'm about to share can be implemented when you do have time with your children.

Parenting 101

In the testimony I just shared, we find a wealth of principles that are involved in godly child-raising. Let's analyze this father's parenting process and see how we can benefit from his example.

The importance of instruction—This man's father did not abdicate his role and responsibility of teaching and training his children. As you probably noticed, his sessions with his family were not heavy-duty, formal teaching times. No, his sessions simply involved taking the time to sit down with his children to read, talk, and discuss the issues of life.

This story also illustrates that Christian fathers don't need to have a Ph.D. in education or Bible to give instruction to their children. In fact, the Christian worker went on to say that his father had no more than an eighth-grade education!

Teaching is an important obligation that you and I have as fathers. Our faithful instruction helps ensure that the next generation carries on our faith in Christ and our biblical values (again, Lord willing). Moses said it this way to the Israelites just before they entered God's Promised Land: "These words which I command you today shall be in your heart. You shall teach them *diligently* to your children" (Deuteronomy 6:6-7). In other words, the parents were to make an all-out effort to pass on to the next generation the faith that had been handed down to them.

And Christian father, that is your mandate as well! Think about it: The Christian faith is, humanly speaking, only one generation away from extinction. Let's make sure we do our part to instill the teachings of our Christian faith to our children and then trust God to do His work in their hearts.

The importance of a personal love for God—The Christian worker who shared his testimony had a love for God that was alive and vibrant. Why? Partly because such a love was modeled for him by a father who had experienced God's love in his own life. Looking again at the exhortation of Moses, note a parent's first responsibility:

> *You* shall love the LORD your God with all *your* heart, with all *your* soul, and with all *your* strength. And these words which I command you today shall be in *your* heart (Deuteronomy 6:5).

Dad, you cannot impart to others what you do not possess yourself! Moses told the *parents* to first love God themselves. *Then* they were to pass their faith on to their children. Make it your chief aim in life to develop a living and growing love for God. Your children will notice and respond to what's important to you.

The importance of environment—Practically every
man has heard of Mickey Mantle, one of the greatest baseball players who ever lived. I certainly heard about him
while growing up. In fact, Mickey Mantle was born and
raised in the small town just north of my hometown of
Miami, Oklahoma. On one occasion, Mickey was actually
in the one and only sporting goods store in Miami during
the off-season. I just happened to be in the same store that
day and, of course, I recognized him right away. I was in
such awe of him that, rather than ask for his autograph, I
casually walked by and purposefully touched his hunting
jacket from behind. I vowed I would never wash that hand
again!

Well, back to my point...

From the time Mickey Mantle was a little boy of five,
his father surrounded him with a life of baseball. Mickey
ate, drank, and slept baseball. In fact, his achievements as
a baseball player were partly attributed to the environment
created by his father. In later life, Mickey credited his
father's constant emphasis on baseball as the strongest
contribution to his Hall-of-Fame success.

Friend, whether it's baseball or Christianity, I think by
now you can see that the atmosphere in your home will
create an impression on your young ones. Your job is to
make sure you establish an environment where your
Christian beliefs and character are on constant display
before your children.

The father in our illustration at the beginning of this
chapter created a climate of love, biblical teaching, and
awareness. The children, at least for that one hour each
day, were surrounded by and enveloped in the love of a

caring, believing father. Going back again to Moses' talk with God's people, note the kind of environment Moses said was to be created by the parents:

> These words which I command you today....You shall teach them diligently to your children, and shall talk of them when you sit in your house, when you walk by the way, when you lie down, and when you rise up. You shall bind them as a sign on your hand, and they shall be as frontlets between your eyes. You shall write them on the doorposts of your house and on your gates (verses 6-9).

Fellow father, you and I need to take these same admonitions to heart. Our children must never for a moment think that our faith isn't the most important thing in our life. They must never for a moment think that the Christian faith is only a "Sunday faith." Instead, they must hear us constantly talking about Jesus. They must consistently see the vibrancy and excitement of our love for Jesus Christ as it is lived out in every aspect of our lives.

> Every golden minute spent with your children accumulates to become your greatest investment and will reap your greatest dividends.

The importance of time—Time seems to be in such short supply for us men! We never seem to have enough of it. We are usually busy every spare minute and second of our time. But be encouraged. No one else has any more time than you do. We all have 24 hours, 1,440 minutes, 86,400 seconds each day to spend as we choose.

Now notice again how the wise father in the minister's testimony chose to spend just one of his hours each day. To him, 60 minutes of time spent with his children was critical. And I'm sure you'll agree that his time was most meaningful to his son as well. This pastor was greatly impacted by a father who "made time" for his children.

Christian dad, there is always time for what you think is important! Therefore, evaluate your time. What in the world is more important than your children? When it comes to the priority of time with your children, I often quote and paraphrase these words spoken by Jesus: "For what is a man profited if he gains the whole world, and loses or forfeits [his children]" (Luke 9:25 NASB). The world doesn't offer enough gold to exchange for your children! You simply must make time for them. Every golden minute spent with your children accumulates to become your greatest investment and will reap your greatest dividends.

The importance of discipline—Up to this point we've looked at the life of one man and his relationship with his father. We have gained some great insights into the biblical parenting process. But branching out from this example, we need to consider at least one more aspect to our parenting—that of disciplining our children.

The Bible repeatedly stresses the need for us to discipline our offspring. For example, Proverbs 23:13 says, "Do not withhold correction from a child, for if you beat him with a rod, he will not die." If this proverb seems a bit harsh for today's society, listen as the Bible compares God's discipline of *His* children with our responsibility to discipline *our* children: "My son, do not despise the chastening of the LORD, nor detest His correction; for whom the LORD loves He corrects, just as a father the son in whom he delights" (Proverbs 3:11-12).

Friend, you and I are rebellious and sinful people. And guess what? Our children are rebellious and sinful too! God has declared, "There is none who does good, no, not one" (Romans 3:12), and that includes our darlings! As God deals with us in our rebellion, we too need to deal with our children in theirs. And like God, who administers His discipline in love, we too must administer discipline in love.

I don't know about you, but administering discipline has never been a favorite thing on my "to-do list" from God. Left to myself, I would probably live out the joke that quips, "Everything in our houses today are run by switches except the children." But you and I can't "wimp out" and delegate that responsibility to our wife or forget it altogether. She can certainly assist, particularly in our absence. But ultimately you as the father are responsible to God for the discipline of your children.

Christian father, God loves you and disciplines you accordingly. So "go thou and do likewise." But heed the advice of these two scriptures as you follow through on God's plan for disciplining your children:

> Fathers, do not provoke your children, lest they become discouraged (Colossians 3:21).

Fathers, do not provoke your children to wrath,
but bring them up in the training and admonition of the Lord (Ephesians 6:4).

The importance of example—It's been said, "Until a
boy is 15 he will do what his father says; after that he does
what his father does." What a description of the power of
example! I know this was sure true in my life. Many of the
good qualities in my life were instilled by my father. I owe
him a great debt of gratitude, and I only wish he were here
so I could express my gratitude.

But there was also a negative side to my dad. This was
understandable because he was not a believer. From what
I observed, I think he and my mother had a good relationship with each other. But on occasion, my father treated
my mother in gruff and disrespectful ways that I determined I would never do when I got married. Well, guess
what? I did them anyway! Such is the power of example!
His influence was so great that I ended up one day dealing
with my wife the way my father treated my mother, and I
quickly realized I had to deal with the pattern that had
been instilled by a bad example.

Think back on your own childhood. Think about the
way your father acted toward your mother. Then think
about the way you are treating your wife. Are there any
similarities, either good or bad? Well, think about this:
Your children are watching your behavior. As I copied my
father's behavior and as you may have copied your
father's behavior, so your children will one day copy your
behavior. Can you point to anything they are mimicking

or might mimick later? Selfishness, pride, outbursts of anger, worldliness? Or Christlikeness and biblical virtues?

The most important way you can be a good example as a father is to accept Jesus Christ as your personal Savior and confess Him before others, including your family, and live a dedicated life for Christ. That's a life worth imitating! Hopefully your family will never ask the question one little girl did:

> **Your consistent, godly example will go a long way in giving children the courage to stand tall for Christ in this evil day.**

A father once took his little girl on his lap and described what a Christian looked like. When he was finished, the little girl looked up at her father with a furrowed, quizzical little face and asked a question that pierced her father to the core, "Daddy, have I ever seen one?"

Christian father, what are you modeling to your children? Are they able to observe what a Christian looks like through your conduct around the house? My friend, ask God to work in your life. Then do everything in your power to be a consistent example of what a Christian looks like. May you so model Christlikeness before your children that in years to come they will stand tall for Christ before their children. Such is the importance of example.

Be Careful...Because the Days Are Evil

There's no doubt we are living in a day of rampant evil. Society is going downhill fast, and it is trying to take us and our families down with it. Yet this is nothing new. The apostle Paul described *his* day as evil (Ephesians 5:16). But he offers us advice that was good in his day and is equally appropriate for ours: "See then that you walk circumspectly [with great care], not as fools but as wise, redeeming the time, because the days are evil" (Ephesians 5:15-16).

From my pastoral and personal experience, I see that many of us Christian fathers today have two main problems. First, as fathers we are not walking with great care. We are not being careful enough about how we act around our children. Our kids sometimes don't see a significant difference between our actions and how those in the world act. That's why Paul says, "Be careful how you walk" (verse 15 NASB). As I said earlier, your consistent, godly example will go a long way in giving children the courage to stand tall for Christ in this evil day.

And second, we as believing dads are not "redeeming the time" (verse 16) when it comes to our children. We are so concerned (and rightly so) about providing for the physical needs of our children that we don't always give proper attention to their spiritual, mental, and emotional needs. The wise father "understand[s] what the will of the Lord is" (verse 17) and works at his role as a dad.

So let me mention the key points again—example, time, discipline, and instruction are what God asks you to focus on as a father so your children can better weather the storm of this present evil day. Such hands-on involvement is a significant part of God's will for you as a parent. God's will is that you never give up on your children. The day is evil and the stakes are high—too high!—for you to fail to give the raising of your children your all.

One pastor who has counseled many young people who have gone astray—even in the area of becoming homosexuals—makes this strong statement about his experience:

> Let me shoot straight with you. If we will function as the loving heads of our homes, respect and love our wives, and follow the guidelines of Ephesians 6:4, our children will not grow up to be homosexuals. I pastored for ten years in the San Francisco Bay area and counseled with more than a few homosexuals. Without exception, every one of them came from a home where the basic principles of Ephesians 5:22–6:4 were not implemented.[14]

That's a pretty strong statement! The strength of this conclusion from Steve Farrar, a writer and men's conference speaker, should give us hope...but it should also motivate us to carry out our responsibilities. He writes that if you and I will follow God's plan and fulfill His will for us as husbands and fathers, we are well down the road, humanly speaking, to better protecting our children in these desperate times. May we stay true to our mandate as leaders in our homes. May we make sure we spend life-changing time with our children. May we be intent on modeling Christlikeness. May we be faithful to teach the truths of Scripture...no matter what!

Walk as Wise Men

I don't know about you, but Steve's words really hit me hard. We dads know what the Word of God says we should do: We are to "walk, not as unwise men, but as wise" (Ephesians 5:15 NASB). But somehow it's easy for us to get sidetracked by all that's going on around us. Then we end up making some unwise decisions about the priority of our children. Let's determine right here, right now, that with God's help, we are going to start making wiser decisions when it comes to our children.

You may be thinking, *But Jim, you don't know the mess I have made of things. I've had my priorities in all the wrong places. I've already alienated my children because of the way I've behaved. In fact, I don't even know where to begin making things right.*

Well, brother, you have *already* started making things right! You are *asking* the questions that show your concern. And you are *still* reading this book. You are *definitely* moving in the right direction toward becoming all that God desires of you—a husband after His own heart.

So now it's time for you to ask God to give you renewed energy as you seek to become a *father* after His heart. Ask for His forgiveness for all the past mistakes you have made. Then go a giant step further and talk to some very special people—your children and your wife—and ask their forgiveness for your lack of love and concern for their welfare. Start fresh today on parenting your children and becoming a man after God's own heart in your role as a family man. I know you can do it! How can I say that? Because God promises to help you to do His will!

The Potential Rewards

Let me close this chapter with an understatement: "Parenting is one of the hardest things you will ever do." If you are a parent, you understand what I am saying. Parenting is not easy. In fact, it is downright hard! But if you will hang in there with God, if you will do your part in parenting your children God's way, and if you will resist caving in to the pressures of society (and even your own children), you will experience incredible blessings from your children. Elizabeth and I know this to be true. We probably made about every mistake that could be made in parenting. And we traveled some rocky roads with our girls. But with God's wisdom from His Word and the wise guidance of others, we kept on looking to God for His help and doing our part according to the Bible. One blessing we now enjoy is joining arm-in-arm with our daughters and their husbands to go about the business of raising another generation—our grandchildren—who (Lord willing and by His grace!) will one day know and love our Savior.

What joy can be experienced by both you and me if we will follow God's plan for parenting! I believe the apostle John said it best:

*I have no greater joy
than to hear that my children walk in truth.*
3 JOHN 4

Little Things That Make a Big Difference

1. Discipline with consistency.

You and your wife come into your marriage from different backgrounds and from different ways of doing all kinds of things. So when you have children, you each tend to discipline from your particular perspective or experience. That's fine if you're both on the same page. But what if you're not? Then there's a potential for conflict. And in the end, your children are the losers if there is tension between you and your wife or inconsistency in methods you use when it comes to disciplining them. Why not sit down with your wife and together map out a strategy for consistent discipline? If you need help, ask others, or take some parenting classes as a couple at your church. Such counsel and classes will guide both of you toward creating consistent biblical principles for child-raising.

2. Pray for your children.

Do the same thing you did with your wife—take pictures of your children with you to work and place them where you can see them throughout the day. Again, as with your wife, when you look at any of the pictures, shoot up a prayer to God for that child and what he or she might be doing right at that moment. With a mentality of praying always

(Ephesians 6:18) for your children, you can't help but be a godly parent. And one more thing—how many others are praying specifically for your children? You and your wife might be the only two people who faithfully pray for them. Don't miss out on this important ministry.

3. Take your children to church.

Going to church is one of the most significant ways to visibly show your children your faith. If you are excited about church and you talk all week about going there, your children will come to see church-going as part of their life as well. You are the leader of your family, and your faith will shape the religious thinking of your children. As you model your Christian faith while taking your family to church, your children will receive a portion of the training they need to understand what it means to have a relationship with Jesus Christ.

4. Invest in your children's future.

"How time flies!" is an expression that especially holds true when it comes to your children. Why, it was only yesterday that you were holding them in your arms...and now they are finishing high school! You want them to be prepared for the future and that usually means further education, whether it's vocational training or going through college. That means you need to start preparing for their future now, because...time flies! Just as you have invested in their spiritual future, now it's time to invest in their mental and physical future.

Education is expensive, and the costs can seem overwhelming. Many fathers give up and hope their children can get student loans, and that's a good resource. But if at all possible, don't saddle your kids with a debt they'll be paying for many years to come. Why not do your children a favor and give them a fighting chance at further education by "socking" a little money away each week or each month until it's time for the training that's needed after high school? Whatever you can do will be much appreciated. One day your children will rise up and called you blessed.

5. Develop father-child traditions.

It's funny what your children remember from their childhood. You quiz them about the past, and they can't remember the things that you thought were highlights, like their birthdays or even gifts that you thought were special. What they really remember are those special traditions that you established, like your annual backpacking trip with your boys, or those monthly "date nights" with your girls. Develop these kind of traditions with your children and you will have no trouble talking with them. Why? Because you will have created an environment that will make them comfortable in baring their souls to you. And all you have to do is give them your time...and, of course, a listening ear.

8

Extending Love
to Family

If it is possible, as much as depends on you,
live peaceably with all men.
ROMANS 12:18

My father-in-law, Henry, was a great guy. He was born in a dug-out cabin in West Texas at the turn of the century. He worked his way through college in the days when most people weren't even graduating from grade school. Working his entire life as an underpaid school-teacher in Oklahoma, Henry probably never made more than $20,000 per year. Yet incredibly enough, he put four children through college. Yes, Henry was quite a man.

But in the winter of his life, Henry developed several kinds of cancer. All of Henry's children wanted him to come live with them, but being a homebody, Henry chose to stay close to home and eventually went into a nursing home in his longtime hometown. Two of Elizabeth's brothers lived fairly close by so they could stay with their dad on the weekends. But the weekdays were a problem. It was after much prayer that Elizabeth and I determined that her father shouldn't be alone during the week.

So we agreed that Elizabeth would fly from Los Angeles to Tulsa, Oklahoma, every Monday morning, and then fly back to our home in California on Thursday evenings or Friday mornings. Little did we know that this weekly visit—and Henry's life—would last for almost an entire year as Henry's health slowly but steadily declined. Obviously, this was a season in our lives when Elizabeth was free to be with her dad. Our girls were married, our nest was empty, and I supported her in her care of her father.

I am relating this story because it provides a perfect illustration of what it means to "honor your parents" and the strain that is often involved in loving your extended family.

I'm sure you have noticed by now that all the topics we have been addressing in this book *really* matter in your marriage! And just like the other issues we've discussed thus far, this issue of extended family—parents, siblings, and in-laws—can be a source of friction and conflict in a marriage. You may have the greatest parents and the greatest in-laws in the world. If so, be sure to thank the Lord daily for your family, because there are a lot of men who don't have good relationships with one or both sets of parents, not to mention their siblings and siblings-in-law!

As we consider what it means to extend our love to family members, I want us to look at one man who did have a good relationship with his in-laws so we can see how we can make the best of this area of our life and our marriage.

The First Law with a Promise

It is estimated that there are as many as 30,000 promises in the Bible. Many of them, to be sure, are specific promises to specific people or specific groups of people, such as the nation of Israel. But there is one particular promise from God that is for all people for all time— a promise given as part of the Ten Commandments: "Honor your father and your mother, that your days may be long upon the land" (Exodus 20:12). The apostle Paul called this "the first commandment with promise" (Ephesians 6:2)

God promises (and God cannot lie—Titus 1:2) that if we honor and respect our parents, He will bless us. And I believe that once we marry, this promise applies to both sets of parents—yours and your wife's. Now I must quickly say that we should honor our parents for the Lord's sake, not just to receive blessings. But it's nice to have God's special blessings as a result of our obedience. Do you desire God's blessings on your life and marriage? I know you do...and so do I! Well, the promise "that it may be well with you and you may live long on the earth" (Ephesians 6:3) is ours...*if* we will honor our parents.

The Law Lived Out

Exactly how do we honor our parents?

As I thought about this question, I thought of Moses. He is one of the greatest men in the Bible—a real man's man. Moses was asked by God to lead a nation of over two million people. He talked face to face with God. He received the Ten Commandments...and on and on his list of privileges goes.

But Moses also gave us a great model of how we should extend love to our family. And by family, I mean our extended family. So, as we search for the answer(s) in the verses below, remember that Jethro was Moses' father-in-law. Also remember that I am using *parents* and *in-laws* interchangeably as we look at what I believe God would ask of us in loving our family, including our in-laws!

Show humility toward your parents—At one point in my married life I entertained the idea of working for my dad, who owned a farm equipment dealership in Oklahoma. Looking back now at that option, it is good that it didn't work out and that our family stayed in California. But working for your parents or in-laws can be a challenge for you, and it can be a strain on your marriage.

Moses, you will remember, married Jethro's daughter and came into the family business of shepherding. After 40 years of serving his father-in-law, God met Moses at a burning bush (Exodus 3:2) and asked him to make a career change (Exodus 3:10). Notice the humility in Moses as he makes his request to leave his father-in-law: "Please let me go and return to my brethren who are in Egypt, and see whether they are still alive" (Exodus 4:18).

The lesson that Moses teaches us here is that courtesy toward our family, whether we work for them or not, is not to be overlooked. Just because we desire to leave their employment or vicinity or we have an important decision to make doesn't mean we can treat parents or in-laws with disrespect. Even with a "divine call" from God, Moses, at close to 80 years old, still came to Jethro with a humble heart and a servant attitude. Moses gave his reasons, not *telling* of his intentions to leave, but *asking* for permission to leave.

Humility sometimes comes hard for men. But by God's grace, you and I can follow Moses' example. And we would do well to follow it, whether it has to do with our parents, or our wife and children, or making requests from our boss at work. Moses teaches us how to have a humble attitude: give your reasons, and ask...not tell.

Honor your parents—Moving along in the story about Moses and his in-laws, we come next to a time after God's people made the exodus out of Egypt. Jethro had decided it was time to bring Moses' wife and her children to meet up with their husband and father. Notice how the great leader of a nation of two-million-plus people greets his father-in-law: "Moses went out to meet his father-in-law, bowed down, and kissed him" (Exodus 18:7). Admittedly, some of Moses' actions depict the cultural traditions of his day, but his example is quickly validated for us today through the Ten Commandments when we read the fifth one, which charges us to "honor your father and your mother" (Exodus 20:12).

> We honor our parents by thinking of them, praying for them, and communicating with them as often as we can.

Christian man, how are you doing at honoring your parents and your wife's parents? This command is not an option or a suggestion. No, it is a command shot straight from the heart of God. How can we show honor to our parents? Read on as Moses shows us how he honored his father-in-law.

Communicate with your parents—After Moses honored Jethro, we see him ask questions about the welfare of his father-in-law. The Bible reports, "They asked each other about their well-being, and they went into the tent" (Exodus 18:7). In other words, Moses was interested in Jethro and communicated it. What is your interest level in your parents and in-laws? Do you care at all? Do you communicate your concern for them, their interests, and their health? Do you personally call or write? Or do you delegate any and all communication with all parents to your wife? Are you so busy doing your own thing that you don't even think about your parents, and never think to communicate with them?

God says that we as men after His own heart should honor our parents and parents-in-law. We honor our parents by thinking of them, praying for them, and communicating with them as often as we can. And when we show such honor, God will bless us.

How does He bless us, you might ask?

- ✑ We are blessed with the wisdom of life experiences. My wife's father, Henry, lived a long time, and I was privileged to sit at his feet and learn from the lessons he learned during his long life.

- ✑ We are blessed by the friendship of our parents and parents-in-law. Henry, as he wanted to be called, was not only my father-in-law, but also a good friend.

∞ We are blessed with the love our parents show to their grandchildren. What a joy it was to take our children back to Oklahoma and have Elizabeth's parents dote over the girls.

All of this is possible, my friend, when we stay in touch with our parents. And the principle of honoring our parents through communcation is especially important when you don't live near your parents. Distance may separate, but communication unites.

Be friends with your parents—The next time you have a chance, read what happened after Moses and Jethro greeted each other and went into Moses' tent (Exodus 18:8-12). But until then, let me give you the abbreviated version. These two men, related only by marriage, appeared to be the greatest of friends as Moses described to his father-in-law the exodus of God's people and the defeat of Pharaoh's army. In turn, Jethro praised God for the miraculous deliverance of the Israelites from bondage. What a scene that must have been as these two men—a father- and son-in-law—spent time with each other, time that focused upon rejoicing in God together. How close are you to your parents? Do you share with your parents what's happening in your life? A phone call once in a while would be nice, but spending time with your parents in person will take your relationship with them to a deeper level.

Listen to your parents—Another way you and I can honor our parents is to ask for and listen to their advice. Whether they are Christians or not, they have a perspective—based on experience—that many times can be helpful. Look at Moses' example again. On the next day after Moses and Jethro had met and spent time together, Moses went to his work as a judge and listened all day long to the people. Then Jethro, who had watched his son-in-law the entire day, made this observation:

> The thing that you do is not good. Both you and these people who are with you will surely wear yourselves out. For this thing is too much for you; you are not able to perform it by yourself. Listen now to my voice; I will give you counsel (Exodus 18:17-19).

How would you respond (or should I say react?) to someone—especially a father-in-law—trying to tell you how to run your business or ministry? "Didn't I start this company and build it from the ground up?" Or, in Moses' case, "Wait a minute! Which one of us was commissioned by God to lead this company of people? If I need your advice, I'll ask for it. Otherwise, mind your own business!" These are the kinds of responses we sometimes have (or at least think in our minds) when someone tries to give us unsolicited advice.

How did Moses respond to his father-in-law's advice? He listened. And then Moses went one step further and "heeded the voice of his father-in-law and did all that he had said" (verse 24). Moses carried out Jethro's advice to the letter! Now I ask you: How are you at listening to the advice, both solicited and unsolicited, of your parents and in-laws? Moses was not too proud to take the advice of another. Perhaps he was able to receive Jethro's advice in a positive way because they had such a good relationship.

Their strong friendship probably made it easier for Moses to accept Jethro's advice.

Don't you see what a great resource God can offer you through your parents and in-laws? Like Jethro and my father-in-law Henry, they have so much to offer! The wisdom gained by honoring, listening to, and heeding their advice might in some way even prolong your life, as the fifth commandment states: "Honor your father and your mother, that your days may be long upon the land" (Exodus 20:12).

In-laws...or Out-laws?

What a great example God gives us of a healthy family relationship in Moses and his father-in-law! Everyone benefitted from their bond. But what about the relationship that isn't ideal? What are some things that hinder or impede a solid friendship between you and your parents and in-laws? As we look at the following possible hindrances, realize that few, if any, of these impediments are insurmountable barriers to a healthier association with your family members. I know I have been guilty of using some of these hindrances as excuses rather than seeing them as opportunities for God to work in me and my family.

Distance—When my wife was growing up, her grandparents lived 30 miles away. Once a year her parents took her and her brothers to see the grandparents. Unfortunately, Elizabeth has no memories of the grandparents coming to see her parents and her brothers. As a result, Elizabeth never really knew her grandparents. Thirty miles away and yet they were complete strangers! Distance is not always measured in miles. Sometimes it's measured in importance.

Absence—Distance can be a legitimate reason for absence. But I confess that even when I lived in the same town as my parents, I rarely went to see them. I would always excuse myself with pious explanations like, "I'm busy doing the Lord's work." Or, "They know that I love them even though I don't get around to seeing them." Well, my friend, I was failing to honor my parents. What excuse are you using for your absence?

Selfishness—Relationships take time. For most of us, time is something we think we don't have. But there is always enough time to do what we want to do...and need to do. We manage to find time to travel, dabble with hobbies, watch the national average of 6.4 hours of television per day, and a myriad of others things. Why? Because we want to do them. We selfishly fail to follow the advice of the apostle Paul: "Let each of you look out not only for his own interests, but also for the interests of others" (Philippians 2:4). Let's find ways to look out for the interests of our parents. God says it is important to honor our parents, and we should see it as important, too.

Manipulation—I have loved studying the relationship that Moses had with his father-in-law. Moses seemed to be the perfect son-in-law—he was polite, respectful, eager to take advice, etc., etc. But Jethro was a pretty good father-in-law himself. Scripture seems to indicate that Jethro came to see Moses for the purpose of bringing Moses' family back. When his mission was completed, Jethro "went his way to his own land" (Exodus 18:27). Jethro came, gave advice, and left. He didn't try to control or manipulate the family in any way.

Now, how about your marriage and the parental relationships on both sides? Some parents become pretty slick at plying manipulation. Perhaps you want to honor your parents and you want to be with them...but because of their constant demands, you find yourself resisting and avoiding them. Clearly you and your wife need to recognize what is happening in your relationships with your parents and agree on how to handle it. And, depending on whose parents are causing the problem, you or your wife may need to talk to that set of parents. But, no matter what happens, you still need to honor and respect them.

> You can't change another family member's heart toward you, but you can surely change yours.

And one last thought: Maybe all of their scheming is a sign that you are not visiting with them as much as you should. In many cases your parents are just wanting to see you, their kids, and those beautiful grandchildren!

How's Your Heart?

Isn't the study of the relationship between Moses and Jethro a refreshing model for us as men to follow in extending love to our family? Their friendship gives you and me great principles about how to live out God's command to honor our parents on both sides and extend His love to them.

It's sad to have to say that most family relationships are not what God desires them to be. Many times we do things that hurt our parents or family members. And, at other times, one of them does something to hurt us. That's often the way it is in a family. And that's also the way alienation begins. I recently heard of a mother and daughter who hadn't spoken to each other in over 30 years. What a loss for those two family members! And compounding this tragic sin were the many grandchildren who had never seen their grandmother, not to mention a grandmother who had never seen her grandchildren. Again, what a loss!

Dear friend, don't let this happen in your marriage. You can't change another family member's heart toward you, but you can surely change yours. Ask God to warm your heart toward your family members. Take Paul's advice to heart: "If it is possible, as much as depends on *you*, live peaceably with all men" (Romans 12:18). And remember, "all men" includes your family and in-laws! Then go the next step and make things right between you. Maybe God has been working in their heart, too!

No one is perfect...so accept the fact! No matter what is going on in your family relationships, *you* can be the mature one who chooses to have a heart of forgiveness. *You* can be the one who prays for your loved ones. *You* can be the one who reaches out and makes an effort to have God's kind of relationship. And don't forget, *you* can draw upon the resources of prayer, the Bible, and the power and fruit of the Holy Spirit (Galatians 5:22-23). By God's grace, *you* can extend love to your family!

Little Things That Make a Big Difference

1. Pray for your parents.

By now your office desk is getting a little cluttered with pictures, but one more won't make a big difference. So put a picture of your parents—and even your wife's parents—on your desk. Again, as you see their pictures, pray for them. Pray for their salvation, if they're not believers. Pray for their health. Pray for other needs they may have. Pray for a good relationship with them as family. Pray for their role as grandparents to your children. And pray for more ways to love and honor them. The point is to find prompts, like pictures, that will help you to think about your parents, and thinking should always lead to praying for them.

2. Stay in touch.

In addition to thinking about and praying for your parents, you should pick up the phone and call them often. Ask how they are doing and how you can pray for them. Also let them know that you are praying for them. Stay in touch by sending postcards while you are on business trips. Send postcards while on your family vacation. The postcards will do two things. First, they will let your parents and in-laws know you are thinking about them. But also, they will keep them up to date on what's going on in your lives. I'm sure it's hard for you to keep up with your own schedule, let alone keep your family up on the latest news. Postcards are a quick way to serve both purposes.

3. Visit your parents.

Each generation of parents has viewed travel differently. So don't wait for your parents to come to you. Instead, go to your parents (with their permission and prior arrangements, of course! No surprise visits!). It's not that they don't love you or don't want to see you and the grandchildren. It's just that they view travel, especially air travel, differently than most of their children. Therefore, plan for trips to visit your parents. If a trip means saving money for weeks or months, then start saving. You honor your parents by visiting them. And through visits, your children can develop meaningful relationships with their grandparents. Your efforts, the memories created, and the friendships built will be worth every penny!

4. Seek parental advice.

The Bible says you and your wife are to leave your parents and cleave to each other when you marry. That means you are to start your own household. It also means you become 100 percent responsible for your own family and the decisions you make. But that doesn't mean that your parents and in-laws don't have some words of wisdom to contribute to the decision-making process. They will feel honored when you seek their advice...and you will become much wiser.

5. Don't delegate "parents" to your wife.

It's so easy to delegate any and all of your involvement with your parents and hers to your wife. After all, you're a very busy man! So you assign your wife to write the notes, create the plans, and make all the phone calls. Besides, both sets of parents think the world of your wife. But as much as they like her, you are still their son and son-in-law, and your contact with them will truly speak volumes concerning your love and interest toward them. You put important business contacts in your notebook for continued follow-up, so why not have all your parents' phone numbers and addresses handy so that wherever you are, you can personally call or write? Some people in your life are too important to delegate all their care to others. Your parents—and your in-laws—should be at the top of your list!

6. Send lots of pictures.

Think a minute about your poor parents. You don't want them to be shocked about how much growth has passed by the next time they see you and/or your children, do you? Then make sure you send a steady stream of pictures their way. Chronicle in print the adventures you and your wife go on, the home improvements you are making, the new car you finally purchased, and the children's growth and activities. Commemorate your vacations by developing three sets of your photos, and send a set to each of your parents. Photos tell your parents and in-laws you are thinking of them and allow them to be with you at least in spirit, if not in person. From your parents' perspectives, no price can be put on a photo of you and your wife and family. Remember, one picture is worth a thousand words...and you know how you hate to write!

9

Tending Your Career

If anyone does not provide for his own,
and especially for those of his household,
he has denied the faith
and is worse than an unbeliever.
1 TIMOTHY 5:8

As a pastor I've met a lot of "Joes"—Joes like the one I'm about to describe. This particular "Joe" had come a long way in his Christian faith. He was reading his Bible and taking his family to church on a regular basis. But there was one more area in Joe's life where God needed to perform radical surgery. You see, Joe didn't like his sales job. And Joe was quick to let me and everyone else know that "the customers are fickle, the suppliers are unreliable, and my company is insensitive." Joe was very negative about anything related to his career.

Learning About Your Job

Well, one day Joe was reading in the book of Colossians and came across this verse:

> Whatever you do, do it heartily, as to the Lord
> and not to men, knowing that from the Lord you
> will receive the reward of the inheritance; for
> you serve the Lord Christ (Colossians 3:23-24).

Then, as he had been trained in a "How to Study the Bible" course, Joe read the accompanying cross-reference (another scripture that teaches the same truth) in his Bible. This verse seemed to apply to his job as well:

> Bondservants, be obedient to those who are your
> masters according to the flesh, with fear and
> trembling, in sincerity of heart, as to Christ; not
> with eyeservice, as men-pleasers, but as bond-
> servants of Christ, doing the will of God from the
> heart, with goodwill doing service, as to the Lord,
> and not to men (Ephesians 6:5-7).

By the time Joe finished taking in these verses, he was feeling pretty convicted about his attitude toward his job and his boss. But still wanting to be thorough, Joe read one final reference:

> Therefore, whether you eat or drink, or whatever
> you do, do all to the glory of God (1 Corinthians
> 10:31).

It wasn't long before people started hearing Joe comment on what great customers he had, what wonderful service he was receiving from his suppliers, and what a terrific company he worked for! Who changed? Maybe everyone! Why? Because Joe changed his attitude about his job. He realized that he was working as a representative of Jesus

Christ. Therefore he went to work with a joyous attitude. Yes, Joe had changed, and his change apparently affected everyone else as well. And wonder of wonders, his sales increased!

This story about Joe brings us to our next important priority in the life of a man who desires to be God's kind of husband—that of our career. As I shared about Joe, I didn't say anything about his family, but when he was dissatisfied with his job, his family felt the effects of his discontent. And I don't think Joe's family is unique in being affected by a man's problems at work. How long has it been since you had a "bad day at the office," came home, kicked the dog, yelled at your beloved wife, and ignored your sweet children?

I'm exaggerating of course and I know you don't do this, but I also know that when you and I have a rough day at work, our frustration is usually felt by the others in our home. So it's important that we gain a better understanding of how our jobs and careers fit into God's grand scheme for us as husbands who want to follow after His will. By doing so, we'll become better workers, as well as better husbands and fathers.

Doing God's Will

I'm sorry to continue writing about Joe, but he provides us with such good illustrations for tending our careers! While Joe was reading the passage from Ephesians 6:5-7, right in middle of these verses he noticed the phrase, "doing the will of God from the heart" (Ephesians 6:6). Joe had never before thought about the truth that his job and his attitude toward his job were somehow connected with God's will for his life.

Perceiving God's will—Over the years, men have often come to me and asked how they could "know" God's will. They wanted me to help them "find" God's will for their life. Well, I was happy to tell them then, and you now, that God's will isn't lost. God's will is not some mystical revelation that slowly appears only after many hours of contemplation. No, God's will is right in front of you. God plainly says in Ephesians 6:6 that His will is that you work as if you were doing so for the Lord, not man.

> God's will is that you work as if you were doing so for the Lord, not man.

Pretty simple, isn't it? What an exciting prospect to know that every day when you go to work, you are, in that area of your life, fulfilling God's will. Just the awareness that we're working for God should be enough to keep you and me motivated on the job. But there are some other resons that motivate us, such as...

Providing for your family—From the first day of his creation, man (Adam) was to work. Initially man's work was for God's purposes only, not to provide for himself. That's because God had taken care of man's need (Genesis 1:29). But after man's "fall" into sin, Adam's work took on a much more desperate focus. God said, "In toil you shall eat...all the days of your life....In the sweat of your face you shall eat bread" (Genesis 3:17-19). And friend, Adam's "curse" applies to you and me today as husbands. The responsibility of providing for our wife and any children falls on our shoulders. And as we do our work "heartily, as to the Lord" (Colossians 3:23), our family benefits. We fulfill God's will and as a result, God is glorified.

Proving to be a servant—Throughout my life and my several careers, I have at times desired to be great, not in a domineering way, but in the sense of being good at what I did. First I wanted to be a great pharmacist. Then I desired to be a great salesman. Then I longed to serve God as a great minister, perhaps even as a great Christian leader. Many men believe that greatness comes from having wealth, authority, and power. But true greatness—biblical greatness—comes by being a servant. Jesus' disciples viewed greatness as lordship rather than servanthood. This was the example of their day, and, I think you will probably agree, it is the example of our day as well. Hear Jesus' explanation of what determines true greatness:

> You know that the rulers of the Gentiles lord it over them, and those who are great exercise authority over them. Yet it shall not be so among you; but whoever desires to become great among you, let him be your servant. And whoever desires to be first among you, let him be your slave (Matthew 20:25-27).

Mark it well! Greatness, according to Jesus, comes with being a servant. As you provide for your family, you are serving them. This is your greatest act of service. And your service should extend beyond your family, so purpose in your heart that you will show a servant attitude to everyone you meet on the job. See your career as a unique opportunity to "minister" and give service in the field in which you are most skilled.

Jesus, the greatest man of all, did not come "to be served, but to serve and give His life a ransom for many" (verse 28). Now, that's greatness! May yours be a "service" career. May you put more into the lives of others than you take away.

Proclaiming your faith—When we work for God and the good of our family, and when we serve others, we further fulfill God's will by demonstrating our faith. For most men, including me, sometimes it's hard to be vocal about our Christian faith. If it's hard for you to stand up at the shop and express your beliefs, you'll really benefit from the final chapter of this book, "Reaching Out to Others." But for now, try doing your best to be the best at what you do. Try doing your work "heartily, as to the Lord" (Colossians 3:23). Then when people start standing in line to find out why you are so good at what you do and why you are such a servant, you can tell them it's because of Jesus Christ and His control over your life. This, my friend, is

> Think of your servant attitude and your productivity on the job as a nonverbal platform for quietly proclaiming Christ to a watching world.

what it means to "do all to the glory of God" (1 Corinthians 10:31).

Unfortunately there were some men in Bible times who weren't doing their work heartily. In fact, they weren't even working! They not only weren't providing for their families, but they were a bad testimony to the Christian faith. That's why Paul cautioned all men, "If anyone does not provide for his own, and especially for those of his household, he has denied the faith and is worse than an unbeliever" (1 Timothy 5:8).

As I said, we will consider your verbal witness in a later chapter, but for now I want you to think of your servant attitude and your productivity on the job as a nonverbal platform for quietly proclaiming Christ to a watching world. Jesus said it best: "You are the light of the world. A city that is set on a hill cannot be hidden…. Let your light so shine before men, that they may see your good works and glorify your Father in heaven" (Matthew 5:14,16).

Pursuing your career—Did you know that the word *vocation* comes from a Latin word that means "calling"? In earlier days, men saw their careers as a calling from God. If you and I were to view our careers as a calling from God, we might become a little more excited about making that commute to work each day! This thought takes us right back to the will of God. If you are miserable in your job, like Joe was, or if you are bored in your work or dread going to work each day, then God is speaking to you. Either He wants you to change the job you are in, or more likely, as with my friend Joe and most men, He wants to change your attitude.

"The Grass Is Always Greener…"

Let me ask you a question: Do you know anyone at your workplace, including yourself, who is truly content with their job? I'll bet your answer is probably, "Not many!" In their pursuit of the "American dream," most people are not content with their jobs or even their line of work. In their hearts they may be thinking, *The grass is greener on the other side of the fence*. What are some possible reasons for their dissatisfaction?

A lack of purpose—Friend, apart from Jesus Christ, there is no real purpose in life. Without Christ and without a purpose, a man is merely living out the ancient gladiator's motto, "Eat and drink, for tomorrow we die." But with Jesus as your Savior and guiding force, you have a purpose—"doing the will of God," even in your work. If you are providing for your family, serving others, and working as unto the Lord, then you should be well content with your job. That doesn't mean you won't ever change jobs. It just means that you are happy about where you are for now, and until God's purpose for your life changes. That's contentment.

A lack of understanding—When a man doesn't understand what God desires for his life, he is at risk of falling into the trap of materialism. I know I was lacking understanding in years past. I was "out there" trying to get the "stuff" that I thought would make me happy and my family better off. But the entire time I was frustrated and unhappy. I sensed that something was wrong, but I couldn't seem to get a handle on what that something was. I felt like I was on a treadmill and didn't know how to get off! Understanding that the true purpose of your career is an opportunity for serving God, serving your family, and serving those you work with should make yours a heart of contentment.

A lack of obedience—Still other Christian men have fallen into the trap of materialism for other reasons—they *want* to maintain a lifestyle that pampers their flesh, impresses their neighbors, provides for their desires, inflates their egos, and fulfills their cravings! They like "living in the fast lane." And in many cases, they have pushed everything else aside, including their marriages, in order to succeed in their careers. Even when some of these men are warned of their disobedience by some caring person, they still continue down the path of destruction.

I recently read this tragic story of just such a man as described by a heartbroken friend:

> Just a short time ago I lost one of my best friends to his career. It was devastating for all of us. His career became such an obsession that he lost everything else on his climb to success—his wife, two little children, and his faith. And by the way, he didn't reach success either.... It all began by working more and more hours to climb the career ladder in his company.[15]

The author who shared this story went on to say that his friend had come to him in the middle of his crisis and sought help. But when the author counseled, "The best thing you could do to save your life and your marriage is quit your job. I would rather see you sweeping streets and living in an apartment—back with your family and back in the church—than in the job you now have with all its perks,"[16] sadly, his friend chose his job and ended up divorced from his family and living Satan's lie. The man was a picture of willful disobedience. He had lost sight of his purposes and God's will.

Remembering Your Purpose

I once read a book entitled *God's Forgetful Pilgrims*.[17] That title sure describes my life at one time! Take it from me, it doesn't take much to qualify as one of God's forgetful pilgrims. It's easy to get so wrapped up in our careers that we forget about God and His purpose for our life. Have you had any lapses in your spiritual commitment over the years? Well, thanks be to God that, even though at times we may "forget" Him, He doesn't forget us (Psalm 105:8). But what God *does* forget is our sin: "As far as the east is from the west, so far has He removed our transgressions from us" (Psalm 103:12). Right now is a good time to stop and thank God for never giving up on you. What a great God you and I serve!

Why don't you also make a commitment right now that, with God's help, you won't forget His purpose for your life again? Whatever happened in the past is just that—in the past, and God has forgiven you. Now it's time for you to be desirous of pursuing God's best for your life, and that includes your career. As you make this commitment, you may need to make some drastic decisions regarding your work habits, your attitude toward your job, and your career itself.

Balancing Your Life

If you made a commitment or two concerning your attitude and maybe even the focus of your job and your career, congratulations! Commitments are hard to make, especially if they require turning some things around. But hopefully you did it! Maybe you made a commitment to change your attitude about your work? If you did, it will take strong effort to fight against your flesh while you are on the job. Or maybe you made a commitment to not allow your career to be so all-consuming? In this case, it will take an equal amount of effort to counter your tendency to allow your job to consume you.

Here's the tension as I see it: God wants a husband to provide for his family, proclaim his faith, and pursue God's calling in his career, which means a man must have a right attitude and do his best. But at the same time, God also does not want a husband to work so much that he neglects his relationship with God, or his wife, or his children. Now, how is all of this possible? The answer is this: A husband must apply *balance* to his work life. And how does a husband achieve this balance? Here are a few questions to ask yourself:

- Am I asking God to give me wisdom in achieving balance between my career and my marriage?

- Am I studying my Bible to find out what God says the balance should be?

- Am I continually evaluating my work ethic? Do I give my employer a fair day's work for a fair day's pay?

∽ Am I brave enough to add up the hours I spend commuting to and from work, working on the job, and working at home during a "normal" work week? Does that total reveal whether I've let my job become too all-consuming?

∽ Am I brave enough to ask my wife if she thinks my work hours are out of balance?

∽ Am I brave enough to ask my wife if my attitude about my job is negative and possibly affecting my relationship with her?

∽ Am I brave enough to ask a friend if he thinks my career is out of balance with my home life?

∽ Am I brave enough to ask my boss to give me his assessment of my work ethic and to make suggestions for improvement?

∽ Am I continuing to grow in my present job? And am I growing vocationally to prepare myself for God's purposes for my life in the future, whether that might include a different job or a promotion?

Answering these questions will help you to successfully navigate the minefield every husband must traverse on his way to balancing work and family. Completing this exercise and making the right choices will also pave the way for you to reap many rich blessings!

Reaping the Blessings of Work

"Work," in all its uses, is mentioned over 350 times in the Bible. It is God's will that you and I work. And whatever career you and I believe to be the will of God for our lives will demand hard work to be successful.

Charles M. Schwab, the great steel tycoon, is famous for his "Ten Commandments of Success." What was number one? Mr. Schwab put hard work at the top of the list. He explained, "Hard work is the best investment a man can make."

Thomas A. Edison, the great inventor, denied he was a genius. Instead, he attributed his success to dedicated work. He rarely slept more than four hours a night and was often seen catching a nap or two during the day. Too much sleep, he claimed, "makes you dopey. And you lose time, vitality, and opportunities."

Today, our culture has different ideas about work than in years past. Not only has society slipped in its moral fiber, but it has also slipped in its commitment to excellence in the workplace. Many people either want everything given to them without working for it, or they don't want to work very hard to get it. You, however, as a man after God's own heart, are different. You understand God's purposes and priorities for your life. You are working hard for God and His glory, and not for men. And what kind of blessings can you reap from this kind of obedience in your work?

First, you will be blessed in knowing that you are fulfilling the will of God in your life. That alone should be blessing enough, but there's more...

Second, you will be blessed in knowing that your wife shares God's blessings with you. Think about this: As the head of your home, your obedience or disobedience affects your wife's life as well. That's why your obedience is so critical.

Third, you will be blessed by knowing that you are doing your best as you do your work unto the Lord. You will know the fulfillment that comes from taking pride in the excellence of your work.

Brother, if you work hard, understand the will of God, and live out His purposes and His priorities for your life, you will provide for your family, you will be the best at your vocation, and you will progress in your career. You will be a "light on a hill." And you will fulfill the will of God for your life. These blessings and more will be yours... when you tend to your career *God's* way.

Little Things That Make a Big Difference

1. Be positive.

If you have a job, you have much to be grateful for! It pays the bills, at least your needs, if not your wants. And it may even be a job you like. Plus, if you are constantly learning about your job and how to be better at it, you should always be excited and growing in your work. And besides all of the above, God is your boss (Colossians 3:22-24)! Your office has enough complainers and whiners who hate their jobs and often influence everyone else to be as miserable as they are. So be joyful! It will set you apart and give you an opportunity to share Christ when people want to know why you are so positive.

2. Be on time.

It's been said that 90 percent of success is "showing up." And I might add, showing up early. Being on time is a discipline. Have you allowed yourself to fall into the bad habit of arriving late? Late for work? Late for meetings? Late for doctors' appointments? (You get the point!) If so, then you need to deal drastically with this area of your life. This one discipline will put you at the head of the Career Class. It will also show that you are thinking of others and not yourself. Being on time says I value you and your time. Being on time is also an issue of motivation—self-motivation. Who's in charge of your life and schedule? You are! So first, acknowledge the importance of being on time, both to your career and to your Christian testimony. Then, set all your clocks and watches forward five to ten minutes. That's usually the amount of time most people are late to appointments. (And note: This one "little" exercise will take care of most of your tardiness!)

3. Be a lifelong learner.

Being a learner is not solely about a career. Oh, it will help your career if you are willing to learn new skills related to your job and line of work. But if you are a learner in every area of life, you will always be growing both professionally and as a person. You will see everyone as your teacher— your workmates, your boss, your parents, your educators, and especially your wife. Who better to listen to and learn from than the one who loves you unconditionally, trusts you unwaveringly, follows you loyally, and cares the most about your career? Your wife can be your greatest teacher if you will let her. She can teach you how to love, how to care, and how to serve. All these are important elements needed in a Christian man as he tends to his career—not to mention how important they are to being a husband after God's own heart.

4. Don't procrastinate.

How does the familiar slogan go? "Just do it," and I would add, "Just do it...*now!*" Ask yourself, Why am I putting a project off? Does it seem too over-whelming? Then break it down into bite-size pieces. Or as another saying goes, "How do you eat an elephant? One bite at a time." Are you putting off starting your project because you don't know where to begin and you're too proud to ask? Swallow your pride and ask for advice. Then when you succeed, make sure you give those who advised you credit for their help. Procrastination, like being late, is a bad habit that can be conquered. Here's a suggestion: The next time someone asks you to do something, large or small, sit down and make a list of all the people and materials you will need to complete the project. Then immediately do some-thing, anything, even a "little thing," to get started. That's the momentum you need. Once you've started, you'll find it easier to continue to the finish.

5. Don't bring your work home.

You work hard on your job for eight to ten hours a day. But at the end of the day, there is still more work that could be done. That's a law of all "work"! What's the answer? Bring it home? Wrong! That answer may be good for the company, but it's bad for the family. How many waking hours are you at home anyway? Maybe five or six on a good day? Your wife and children deserve every precious minute of that short time. Don't sell out those few minutes to your company. Leave both your mental and physical work at the office. And here's another law: "Work expands to fill the time allotted to it." Therefore, allot "work" to be done at work. Don't allow yourself to get into the habit of thinking there is always the "home office" as a backup plan when you need to catch up on your time because you talked on the phone too much, went out to lunch with the guys, or spent too much time getting ball scores online while you were at work. Work hard and finish before you start home. Then when you arrive home, your wife and family will have all of you. And don't they deserve that?

10

Making Time for Fun

In case you haven't noticed, this book has included some pretty heavy content and advice. I know I'm repeating myself, but marriage is hard work! Elizabeth and I have been married nearly 40 years, and we still have to work daily on our relationship. We are both highly creative people, and since we work at home as writers dealing with heavy subject matter and constant deadlines, things can get pretty serious. So at times we just stop...and go for a walk in the woods, or putt around the lake in our little boat. Then, if we *really* want to have fun, we will find a bookstore and browse for hours. And more often than not, we make no purchases. You see, the fun was in the looking—looking together.

Now, how about you? Had any fun lately? Before you answer, let me quickly add, Have you had any fun *with your wife* lately? I know a lot of men who are having all kinds of fun. The problem is, none of the fun is with their wife or family...and that's the topic for discussion in this chapter.

God Wants You to Have Fun...Really

Christians, and specifically Christian couples, should have the most fun, laugh the loudest, be the most humorous, and enjoy life more than anybody else. Why? Let's evaluate why you and your wife should be having fun in your marriage.

First, the two of you started your relationship by having fun. That's what dating and building a relationship is all about—building a friendship and enjoying each other's company in the process. You couldn't have been much different than Elizabeth and me. I'm sure that like us, you and your honey took advantage of every opportunity to be together and made those times fun. In fact, you two were having so much fun and enjoying each other's company so much that you decided to get married and continue with the enjoyment! So what happened? Have the cares and burdens of married life "rained on your party"? Then chances are, you or your wife—or both of you—have stopped working at having fun.

Second, the fruit of the Spirit is joy (Galatians 5:22). When you walk by the Spirit as a Christian, there should be joy in your life. Obviously there is the joy of your salvation, the joy of eternal life, and the joy that the Lord is your strength (Nehemiah 8:10). But you should also enjoy the joy of life—of living, and especially the joy that can come from having a lifelong relationship with your wife. I believe that's the emotion Adam experienced when God brought Eve to him. He said, "This is now bone of my bones and flesh of my flesh; she shall be called Woman, because she was taken out of man" (Genesis 2:23). Can you sense Adam's joy? Can you picture the fun that Adam and Eve must have had as they frolicked through the Garden of Eden without a care in the world? If you can remember, that's the same kind of joy you and your wife experienced back in the early days of your marriage!

Third, the Bible says that laughter, mirth, and fun are like medicine. There is health in having a merry heart, in laughing a little and having fun. This is God's prescription for the bittersweet world we live in:

> A merry heart makes a cheerful countenance,
> but by sorrow of the heart the spirit is broken
> (Proverbs 15:13).

> All the days of the afflicted are evil, but he who
> is of a merry heart has a continual feast
> (Proverbs 15:15).

> A merry heart does good, like medicine, but a
> broken spirit dries the bones (Proverbs 17:22).

And *fourth*, there is the joy of being married to the most beautiful and wonderful woman in the world—your wife. You married your wife because you enjoyed being around her. She possessed qualities, gifts, and abilities that you admired. Therefore you wanted to be near her. She brought you joy and happiness. And without getting too personal, I also believe there is the joy of your sexual union. This is the way it should be. God meant for a husband and wife to have fun in their sex life. God repeatedly speaks of the sexual relationship between a husband and wife in a way that suggests that a couple should enjoy each other sexually. For instance,

> Let your fountain be blessed, and rejoice with the wife of your youth. As a loving deer and a graceful doe, let her breasts satisfy you at all times; and always be enraptured with her love (Proverbs 5:18-19).

You'll want to read the book of Song of Solomon in your Bible and get a further understanding of the joy and intimacy God designed for the marriage relationship. Take in God's picture of how much fun He intends for a couple to have, whether it's in the bedroom or out running in a field. Picture the fun Solomon and his bride had as he desired to whisk her away:

> **Life is serious enough, so if you've lost your sense of humor, it's time to go find it!**

> Rise up, my love, my fair one, and come away! (Song of Solomon 2:13).

And sense the anticipation of his bride as she responded,

> Come, my beloved, let us go forth to the field; let us lodge in the villages. Let us get up early to the

vineyards; let us see if the vine has budded, whether the grape blossoms are open, and the pomegranates are in bloom. There I will give you my love (7:11-12).

A Place for Humor

In his epic work on spiritual leadership, J. Oswald Sanders devotes a whole section to humor as an essential quality for leadership and makes this statement:

> Since man is in the image of God, his sense of humor is a gift of God and finds its counterpart in the divine nature. But it is a gift which is to be controlled as well as cultivated. Clean, wholesome humor will relax tension and relieve a difficult situation more than anything else. It can be of untold value in a leader, both for what it does for him and for the use it can be in his work.[18]

Humor, according to Sanders, can play an important role in leadership, whether it has to do with functioning as the spiritual leader at home or leading a board meeting at work. Life is serious enough, so if you've lost your sense of humor, it's time to go find it!

What Happened to the Fun?

Let me pause for a minute and elaborate a bit on what I'm saying: I realize that there is a serious side to life. Whether you or I are an older man or a younger man, we are to be "sober" or "sober-minded" (Titus 2:2,6). Being a husband and leader in our home is a big assignment. We should never take that responsibility lightly. But that doesn't mean fun should be absent from our life, and especially from our marriages. I alluded to this earlier, but I believe that both of us had some great fun during the dating period and as we were courting our wives-to-be. That same atmosphere of fun probably continued for a while into the marriage. But with the passage of time, that fun may have diminished. Which one (or ones) of these "cares" might be taking the joy out of your lives?

- *The press of limited finances?*—It's hard to laugh when there is more month than money. The cares of financial responsibility in a marriage can easily squeeze out all of the wonderful fun you had while you were dating. You can forget that most, if not all, of that fun was free. What can you do to restore that fun? For example, how much does it cost to take a walk in the park?

- *The pull of you both working?*—I know this was a problem when Elizabeth and I first married. Elizabeth worked the day shift, and I worked at night. It's hard to have much intimate fun...or any other type of fun!...when you are never together.

- *The pull of a new baby?*—A couple without children is free to come and go as they please with no commitments. But add a little one, and it seems that a lot of the fun stops. Three A.M. feedings are not fun!

∽ *The pressure of a career?*—In the last chapter, we talked about the pressure that can come from your employer at work. For instance, you may feel as if your company wants you to have your fun at work and not at home, and that the demands of your job end up keeping you away from home. It's also possible that your pressure comes from the fact your wife works too. Then I'm sure you know all too well it's hard to have much fun if your careers keep you separated for much of the time.

∽ *The problem of familiarity?*—(Or should I say, lack of familiarity?) Now...how long have you been married? It seems that as the years go by, a lot of couples spend less time together. If you and I don't make an effort to have fun to keep our marriages fresh and vibrant, they can grow cold. If you and I don't continue to nurture a close relationship with our wives, it's easy to become complacent toward our mates. The great friendship we enjoyed in the earlier years of marriage, with all its fun, can turn into a distant memory. Chances are that if you can't remember the last time you and your wife had some fun together, then you and she are already deep into a stale marriage.

∽ *The predicament of bad health?*—Fun can sometimes be seen as something you do when you are young and healthy. However, fun, joy, humor—whatever you want to call it—is a state of mind, an attitude. If having fun, in all the good senses of the word, is important to your well-being and the well-being of those around you, and especially your wife, then you will cultivate a merry heart. It's contagious! And even when one or both of you are in bad health, fun might just be "what the doctor ordered."

So, once again, what cares might have taken the fun out of your marriage? Did you identify a few? I came up with this list of cares as I evaluated my own life, because these are the cares that have robbed my joy at different times in my marriage. I'm almost sure there are several that you can relate to as well. So the question now is, How can you recapture some of that fun from the past?

Recapturing the Fun

Here's a key thought for you as you are reading this chapter on making time for fun: Ask your wife to share some of the qualities that attracted her to you. I'll bet one of those qualities was your fun-loving nature. Your wife-to-be felt happy around you. You made her laugh. She always knew that the two of you would be having fun on those wonderful dates.

Was I right? It sure was true for me in those dating years with Elizabeth. My nickname was "Smilin' Jim." I was completely happy-go-lucky and made sure every date was a blast! Well, it's now time for you to remember what you did to cultivate fun in your budding relationship with your wife back then. It's time to bring that now-dormant "merry heart" out of hibernation and recapture having fun with your wife!

And as you are remembering how much fun you and your wife had in your earlier years together, remember that fun came with a price—the price of time. You are going to have to be willing to make time for fun. In the past you thought having fun together was important to your relationship with your beloved, so why wouldn't it be important today? I hate to repeat myself again, but as we've agreed in past chapters, if something is important, you will make time for it...and that "it" includes fun.

Where Do I Start?

I hope recalling the enjoyment you and your wife once relished has jogged your memory and whetted your appetite for rekindling the fun in your marriage. But just in case you're feeling a little rusty on remembering *how* you had fun, here are some suggestions.

- To begin the fun, remember some of the things you and your sweetheart did while you were dating. Some of those activities might be a little out of date or physically challenging today or even impossible to repeat, so you might have to improvise a little or modify your choices.

- Next, ask your wife what her idea of fun is. What does she enjoy doing? Where would she like to go? Then make sure you do a few of those things and go to a few of those places (even if it isn't quite as much fun for you!).

- Then ask other men at church what they do with their wives for fun. If you're like a lot of guys, you may not be very creative, so you'll want to get as many suggestions as you can in this area, so that you can...

∽   Follow up and be creative. Surprise your wife with a fun activity as soon as possible. Then continue coming up with ideas for fun on a regular basis. Here are a few to get you started:

Go to a museum together—This may sound rather dull, but if you haven't tried it in a while, give it a shot. (Surely your wife would love to go to the Baseball Hall of Fame or the Cowboy Hall of Fame or the Gene Autry Museum!) Your wife is probably so tired of being the "social coordinator" for the two of you that anything you suggest will be one less thing she has to orchestrate. So, believe me, if you plan it, she will go!

Play games together—Recently Elizabeth and I were at a beautiful hotel. As we walked through the pool area on our way to the hotel's coffee shop, we spied a couple playing cribbage. While other couples silently slept or read on separate lounge chairs, this husband and wife were laughing and talking and having the best of times together while they played their board game. How are your skills at checkers? Why not dust them off this Friday night?

Develop a hobby or sport together—I know many couple-friends who play golf or tennis together. It's their mutual hobby. But your couple-hobby doesn't have to cost anything. How about hiking or power-walking together? Or if one of you can't or doesn't want to be quite that active, try developing a mutual hobby like gardening, antiquing, photography, cooking, or travel, even if it's only day trips around your city or state.

Serve the Lord together—For now, I will mention this joint effort only in passing because we will cover ministering together as a couple in the next chapter. But through the decades of our marriage, Elizabeth and I have had some great Christian fun as we've served together at churches, at camps, and with missionaries around the world. What fun it is to serve the Lord together!

> When you have fun together, your marriage will take on a whole new depth and intimacy.

In fact, it could be the most rewarding fun of all...because it has eternal value and blesses others along the way.

Having fun together is like many of the other things you do in your life—it's hard to start, but once you get going, it's much easier to continue. Take the time and make the effort to start having some fun together again. Then see what a difference it makes in your marriage. When you have fun together, your marriage will take on a whole new depth and intimacy.

What Is the Missing Ingredient?

As I look around and observe the marriages of my friends, my associates, and even my neighbors, I see marriages at different stages and degrees of vitality. Of course, all healthy Christian marriages are functioning on the foundation of a love for Jesus Christ and a desire to serve Him. They are solid unions, as well they should be. There's no excuse for a shaky marriage when Christ is the guiding force for both partners.

But there is an ingredient that is missing in some of these "model" marriages. The partners seem to be merely going through the motions. There's no life or energy in the marriage. Then, on the other hand, there are those couples that are having fun. They are still enjoying each other. They are doing things together, and they are great friends with each other. They are living out the sentiment of the verse that marvels, "This is my beloved, and this is my friend" (Song of Solomon 5:16). And as a result, their marriage is a great advertisement for the reality of the joy of living for and in Christ.

So what is missing in one Christian marriage that is present in another? Why is one marriage so alive, while another just seems to plod along? I'm sure there are many factors that account for the differences in energy and joy between couples. But in some marriages, I'm guessing that the difference just might be the missing ingredient of fun. If you sense that some good, wholesome, Christian fun is lacking in your bond with your wife—the kind of fun we've been exploring in this chapter—then make it a goal to purposefully, willfully, and definitely make time for fun. It will be time well spent!

Little Things That Make a Big Difference

1. Turn the TV off!

Let me qualify this by saying, "Turn the TV off one night a week." Television is a "little thing" that many men have trouble with. Just imagine...before television, couples spent their evenings talking, planning their trips and holidays, reading, and even playing chess, checkers, or other games. The television has snatched all this away and substituted the warmth of personal involvement and fun with impersonal entertainment. Call it a "game night" or a "family night," and plan one night each week during which you purpose to have fun with each other as a couple or with your family—without the distraction of the television.

2. Plan a weekend getaway.

This is a "little thing" that's worth repeating over and over until you begin to understand and appreciate how important these brief times away are. Just think of the fun you had as a couple when you first got married. Your universe was made up of just the two of you, and frequently you were able to spontaneously do some crazy things. But those happy days don't have to be over forever! Plan for a weekend of just such craziness. Get away from the distractions of work and home. Have some fun just being together. This will do wonders for your marriage.

3. Ask your wife for suggestions in the Fun Department.

Your wife also remembers all those fun times you two had together in the early days of your marriage. Ask her for suggestions of what she would like to do for fun on an evening or weekend. She may suggest some activities you wouldn't consider to be fun, but be ready for a little give-and-take. You go shopping at the mall with her, and she goes to the ballpark with you. That's fair, isn't it? But keep in mind that whatever she suggests, it is something that's important to her. And if it's important to her, then it should be important to you!

4. Read a Christian joke book.

"Hey, honey, did you hear the one about...?" Sometimes we have to work at having fun. Life can get pretty serious at times. Reading a Christian joke book primes the pump and helps make life seem a little less foreboding. Reading that joke book together as a couple will be even more fun. As Christians you have the "joy of the Lord" and you and your wife can enjoy such a fun thing as good, clean jokes together and the laughter and intimacy sharing them together ignites. Train yourself to trust God and to look on the lighter side of things when life gets a little too stressful. God is in control, so why worry? Have some fun each day. It's contagious. The first thing you know, both you and your wife are able to laugh more easily, even when times are tough. How does the quote go? "Laugh and the world laughs with you. Cry, and you cry alone."

And P.S.—Memorize some of the jokes and repeat them to your workmates. Share your joy and a little of your fun with others who so desperately need any ray of sunshine in their lives!

5. Plan a fun activity this week.

When was the last time you and your wife went out together? Maybe to a museum? Or for a walk in the park? Even a ball game? Plan to take her somewhere fun this week. She is always under the heavy burden of caring for the family and home. And if she also works outside the home, she is really under the pile. So get her away from some of these cares for a few hours. Take the initiative and plan a night out or a special Saturday adventure. Create some fun for your wife. This will give you both a fresh perspective for when you get back to the routine of home and work.

6. Plan a family vacation.

Notice here that the focus is on *you*. Too many husbands let their wife do all or most of the planning when it comes to the family, including the family vacation. You need to take ownership in the Fun Department. So volunteer to plan the next vacation. Get your wife's input, but plan it yourself. And make sure you plan some fun activities, such as a stop to see the world's largest ball of string, or a tour of the plant that makes Tabasco sauce...or an ice cream parlor! I bet your wife can hardly wait for the fun to begin!

11

Serving the Lord

Choose for yourselves this day
whom you will serve...
But as for me and my house,
we will serve the LORD.
JOSHUA 24:15

Have you ever spent a day with a Christian couple who gave you a giant dose of fresh encouragement? Well, that was the experience Elizabeth and I had recently with our longtime friends Bob and Patty. What an inspiration they were to us as we spent one wonderful day together. Bob and Patty are a special couple—they have faithfully served the "senior saints" at our former church for more than 15 years. In this day of short-term commitments, Bob and Patty are shining examples of faithfulness as a married couple and as Christians.

Several years ago, as Bob was devotedly serving in the church, he was asked to join the staff of The Friends of Israel Gospel Ministry. What a decision he had to make! To join such a ministry would mean taking a substantial pay cut, leaving a secure job of 20-plus years, and starting over in an area of ministry that was foreign to him. Well, as is Bob's usual habit, he prayed long and hard...and determined this opportunity was God's leading in his and Patty's lives together. Three years later, their ministry brought them up to our "neck of the woods" and they wanted to get together with us. And it is Bob I have in mind as our example for our next topic in this book—serving the Lord as a couple.

Fellow husband after God's heart, we are getting near to the end of our time together. I pray that you have been challenged as we have looked at ten of the "12 Things That Really Matter in Your Marriage." So far we've learned about...

> ∽ Growing in the Lord—God's husband follows after God's heart.

> ∽ Working as a team—God's husband successfully leads his marriage "team."

> ∽ Learning to communicate—God's husband keeps the lines of communication open.

> ∽ Enjoying intimacy—God's husband works at loving his wife.

> ∽ Managing your money—God's husband is a faithful steward of God's resources.

> ∽ Keeping up the home—God's husband recognizes his home as a priority.

- Raising your children—God's husband is a godly example to his children.

- Extending love to family—God's husband cultivates a friendship with both sets of parents.

- Tending your career—God's husband works for God, not man.

- Making time for fun—God's husband cultivates a merry heart.

And now my friend Bob is providing us with the eleventh out of 12 "things" that really matter in a marriage—serving the Lord. (And I might add, in this case it's actually Bob *and* Patty...as our topic is serving the Lord *together*.)

Understanding Service

We'll begin looking at serving the Lord together as a couple in a page or two. But first, let's make sure we understand what the Bible teaches about our service.

Our service is expected—Bud Wilkinson, the legendary coach of the football team at the University of Oklahoma from 1947 to 1963, once described the game of football as "50,000 people who desperately need exercise watching 22 men who desperately need rest." Unfortunately that is the situation in most churches today. Spiritually gifted men are sitting in the pews watching a small handful of others serve in the various ministries of the church. Like the 50,000 observers at a football game, too many Christians tend to sit on the sidelines in padded pews and cheer for those who are serving God with all their heart.

My friend, this isn't what God intended the church to be like. As Christians we are saved to serve, and God expects that service. The apostle Paul explained it this way: "We are His workmanship, created in Christ Jesus for good works, which God prepared beforehand that we should walk in them" (Ephesians 2:10). A Christian who isn't serving is as ineffective as a car that's been put on blocks. A car in that position is useless! And speaking of useless, a great violinist, Nicolo Paganini, willed his elegant violin to the city of Genoa, Italy, with one condition—the violin was never again to be used. It was a gift designated for preservation...not for service. But not so for you and me as Christians! We are gifts that God has given to the church for the purpose of rendering useful and beneficial service.

Our service must be undivided—Have you ever tried to work for two bosses at the same time? When I had several jobs during my seminary years, I tried...and it's not easy! Why? Because I tended to prioritize one over the other. I couldn't lean two or three different ways at the same time. Jesus' words about undivided service are true:

> No servant can serve two masters; for either he will hate the one and love the other, or else he will be loyal to the one and despise the other (Luke 16:13).

If you are anything like me, then you are having to choose daily whom you will serve. Will it be the gods of passion and pleasure? The gods of greed? Or will it be the one true God? We need to daily—and even minute by minute—decide which "god" we will serve. I can't help but state again a verse I mentioned in an earlier chapter. Remember Joshua's challenge to the children of Israel and his personal resolve as he spoke to them? May Joshua's heart be yours as well:

> Choose for yourselves this day whom you will serve, whether the gods which your fathers served that were on the other side of the River, or the gods of the Amorites, in whose land you dwell. But as for me and my house, we will serve the LORD (Joshua 24:15).

Our service is to be sacrificial—I love reading about the life of King David in the Old Testament. So many men think that religion is for the "womenfolk," that a real man doesn't need God. But David proved just the opposite. It is abundantly clear that David was a man's man. He wrestled against lions and bears. He took on a nine-foot-tall

Service that counts is service that costs.

giant in battle. He conquered a large area of land. And yet David had a heart for God. He was the original man after God's own heart (Acts 13:22). He was an exceptionally strong man of God with an exceptionally strong faith. That's the kind of balance you and I should desire. I want you (and me) to be a man who loves God supremely, to be a husband who loves his wife passionately, to be a worker and provider who masters his career zealously, and to be a man in the church who serves his God intensely. Now, that's a real man!

Anyway…toward the end of his life, David desired to purchase a particular piece of land to use for offering sacrifices to the Lord. The landowner, however, said in words to this effect, "No way will I take your money! You're the king. Take the land—it's yours!" But David held to his intent and declared, "No, but I will surely buy it from you for a price; nor will I offer burnt offerings to the LORD my God with that which costs me nothing" (2 Samuel 24:24).

> **The hardest part of getting started in service is always willingness.**

Here, David gives us another basic principle about our service to God: Service that counts is service that costs. Think about it. We place less value on things that are given to us than we place on things we have paid for. The only difference in the Christian life is that our salvation didn't cost us anything. Rather it cost God everything, as He sent His only Son to pay the price for our salvation. Now, don't you think you and I should be willing to sacrifice a little in our service to our Lord Jesus Christ, the One who gave so much for us? Paul put it this way: "Present your bodies a living sacrifice, holy, acceptable to God, which is your *reasonable service*" (Romans 12:1).

Our service is to benefit others—Christ's body, the church, functions more fully as you and I serve the other members in the church. God has given us spiritual abilities, or as they are called in Scripture, a "manifestation of the Spirit" (1 Corinthians 12:7). These spiritual abilities are gifts given by the Spirit of God to all believers (verse 11) for the "profit of all" (verse 7). Not only has God generously saved you and me by His grace, but He has also called us to serve Him and to benefit others (Galatians 5:13), and has gifted us with the spiritual ability to do so. What a great God we serve!

Getting Started

If you are already serving God and His people, that's great. Keep it up! But if not, the next question you should ask is, "How can I begin to serve?"

I would say this—first, *be informed*. Read your Bible to get a better understanding of what spiritual gifts are and how they work. Start by reading 1 Corinthians chapter 12 and Romans 12:3-7. Find out all you can about these "abilities." And second, *be willing*. The hardest part of getting started in service is always willingness. God is not going to force you to serve Him. No, serving God is your choice. So what will your choice be? Which brings me to the last step—*be available*.

God used all three of these steps in my life. As I asked the question, "How do I begin?" God brought men into my life who could help me understand and develop the spiritual gifts He had given to me. And once I was willing to serve God, I made myself available to my local church. I started my service by washing pots and pans at the church socials and showing up for "work days" on Saturday mornings. Then, as I became better informed and grew spiritually, I was given other responsibilities. And as I was faithful, God moved me into even greater areas of service. I was willing to serve, and I took the final step and actually made myself available. God then did the rest.

And do you know what was most exciting for me about this whole process? My wife was also learning how to serve. As I was growing in my ability to serve, Elizabeth was also growing spiritually. What a blessing it was to our marriage to grow together and also learn to serve together. Which brings me to another couple who served the Lord together...

A Prime Example

Meet Aquila and Priscilla. We don't have the space to do an entire study on this amazing couple in the Bible, but let me give you a brief overview of their life of service as a couple.

∽ *They were available.* Aquila and Priscilla are mentioned in three different chapters of the Bible.[19] In each instance they were ready, willing, and able to do whatever was needed to help the apostle Paul and further the cause of Christ as the church expanded into new territory.

∽ *They were hospitable.* They housed Paul for over a year when he came to the city of Corinth (Acts 18:1-3). They also opened their home for the new church in Ephesus (1 Corinthians 16:19), and again later in Rome (Romans 16:3-5).

∽ *They were knowledgeable.* Having lived and worked with the great apostle Paul for all those years, I'm sure that Aquila and Priscilla were well versed in Scripture. I can just hear Aquila asking,

"Paul, what does this scripture mean?" On one occasion, a man named Apollos was teaching in the church. As Aquila and Priscilla listened, something didn't seem quite right or was missing in his teaching. So this knowledgeable couple took the preacher aside (possibly for "Sunday dinner") and "explained to him the way of God more accurately" (Acts 18:24-26).

∞ *They were fearless.* Being a Christian in the early days of the church was dangerous. There was much persecution of believers by the Roman government and by local pagan religious groups. Paul himself was often beaten, stoned, imprisoned, and mistreated. Hear his estimation of this amazing couple and their invaluable service as they fearlessly trusted God and withstood persecution: "Greet Priscilla and Aquila, my fellow workers in Christ Jesus, who risked their own necks for my life, to whom not only I give thanks, but also all the churches of the Gentiles" (Romans 16:3-4).

Clearly, both members of this marriage were committed to serving the Lord together. The fact that the great apostle Paul commended them before all the churches is a testimony of the impact that a couple can have as they serve together!

Serving as a Couple

Encouraging Your Wife's Growth

Now, let's fast-forward to your marriage today. Maybe you are a husband whose wife is lagging behind spiritually.

Maybe her lack of interest is due to laziness, or a consuming career, or the constant demands of a "flock" of small children. But whatever the reason, she isn't growing in the Lord.

Now you, on the other hand, are ready to grow...and go! You are excited about reading and studying your Bible. You're wanting to read as many books as you can on Christian living and marriage (like this one!). You're definitely ready for whatever God wants to do with and through you! And you are eager to serve and would love to serve with your wife.

Boy, does this ever sound familiar! I was in exactly this position once myself. Less than a week after Elizabeth became a Christian, I walked into our kitchen and announced, "I think God is calling me into the ministry." Now picture this: My wife was only a few days old in the Lord. She was trying to figure out what it meant to be a Christian, a Christian wife, and a Christian mother all at once. And now I was telling her she was going to be a pastor's wife, too! Well, my eager friend, take a page out of my book. If your wife isn't where you are spiritually or where you think she needs to be spiritually, back off a little. You'll both be glad you did!

Think back on your own spiritual growth. How long did it take for God to get your full attention? One year? Five years? Point made! Be patient with your dear wife. God was certainly patient with you! Start by praying faithfully for her spiritual growth. Be sure you attend church together each week. Encourage her as gently as possible to get into a ladies' Bible study. And be sure you continue on in your own growth. Be the best, most loving and godly husband you can be...and then trust God to do the rest.

Lord willing, one day your sweetheart will sign up for a women's Bible study or in some way indicate that she is ready to start growing. Or maybe, as was my experience with my Elizabeth, she'll walk into the kitchen one day and say, "When are you going to apply for seminary? Didn't you say you wanted to go into the ministry?"

Encouraging Your Own Growth

Now, there is another possible husband-wife Christian-service scenario. And as you read along, realize that this is the situation in far too many Christian marriages. Could it be describing you?

In this scenario, you, the husband, are lagging behind spiritually. Maybe you came to Christ later than your wife did. She's had several years to grow in her faith, and she is already involved in serving the Lord. You, on the other hand, are just beginning, and you're not quite sure what is involved in being a Christian. And as for service, you're scared to death. So what do you do?

Over the years I have observed three responses from husbands who find themselves in this situation.

Response #1: Dropout—The dropout husband sees that his wife is more advanced than he is spiritually and feels like giving up and dropping out. He weakly reasons, *She's so far ahead of me that I'll never catch up. So why try? I'll go to church and learn what I can, but catching up is impossible. And it's also a lot of work! Besides, my job takes too much of my time. I don't have the time to study like my wife does.*

Have you had thoughts like these? Well, you are not alone. There are a lot of other guys who are in this same dilemma. And to compound the problem, most wives with husbands who have withdrawn spiritually start pulling back themselves, waiting and praying that their husbands will "catch fire" and want to start growing and serving the Lord. This husband is *passive* in his support of his wife's service. He is discouraged so he simply drops out of the effort of the Christian race or, at best, puts his Christian life in neutral.

Response #2: Holdout—The second response comes from the husband who is intimidated by the maturity of his wife and becomes so threatened that he actually begins undermining his wife's efforts to serve God. He holds out on growing personally, and selfishly hopes to bring his wife down to his level of maturity (...or should I say immaturity?). This sounds like a tactic an unbeliever might resort to, but I have known Christian men who are guilty of *actively* holding their wives back. In fact, I know one husband who is constantly thinking up projects for his wife to do in order to keep her so busy that she doesn't have time to serve God. His latest project was to buy a business and have his wife run the business while he does "other" things.

Response #3: Step out—This is the husband who makes the right response. He decides that he needs to serve God too and does something about it. He steps out and asks for help from other more mature men in his church. He makes himself available at church and shows up at every opportunity to serve. He decides to start reading and studying his Bible. And he even asks his wife to join him in a ministry as a couple. This is a true husband after God's own heart. He steps out and chooses to serve the Lord.

Serving with All Your Heart

Three men and three responses. Which husband would you say most typifies you? Are you a dropout, a holdout, or a step out?

If you believe in your heart that you are the step-out husband, I want to commend your growth and service. Keep up the good work. Continue serving with all your heart. You are a much-needed breed indeed. May your tribe increase!

And if you answered that you are either a dropout or a holdout, I want to thank you for your honesty. It's hard to admit that you are not where you need to be spiritually. Such admission is a good beginning, because a problem defined is a problem half solved!

So now, my courageous friend, you need to take a bold step and go to your praying wife and be as honest with her as you've been with me. Tell her that, with God's help and her support, you are now desirous of serving the Lord. Ask her to pray for you. Ask her for suggestions on how to begin serving. Then take another bold step and make an appointment with a pastor or a leader at your church and ask about areas where you can begin serving the Lord. Dear brother, if you are willing, you will become a man who is growing in the Lord, loving your wife and family, *and* serving the Lord. You will be a man and a husband after God's own heart!

Bob and Patty. Aquila and Priscilla. These couples are and were sold out in their service to God. May they be an encouragement to you as they have been to me. May you and I have a heart that is sold out for serving our Lord Jesus. And may our hearts for the Lord be so inviting and so irresistible that our wives will gladly join us in serving the Lord.

Little Things That Make a Big Difference

1. Look for opportunities to serve.

Serving others does not come naturally for most people, and maybe especially men. Sometimes we think to ourselves: *God has placed me in a leadership role. And as a leader, others serve me, including my wife...my children...my subordinates at work...even the ministers at church.* Is such reasoning right? No, its wrong! Jesus, God in flesh, the greatest leader who ever lived, didn't think like this or act like this or live like this. He came to serve others (Matthew 20:28). And that should be your mind-set as well.

Ask God to give you a servant's heart. Ask God to open your eyes to just one thing you can do to serve in your church. Help at a work day? Clean up after a social? Work as a helper in a Sunday school class? The task doesn't have to be glamorous or difficult. In fact, the less attractive, the better. Then make sure you are faithful in your service. Remember, it's the Lord Jesus whom you serve (Colossians 3:24).

This chapter has been about serving the Lord, and His people—His people at church. But you are also to serve His people under your own roof—your wife and children. What "little thing" can you do

to serve your wife today? Your children? Either set
of parents?

2. Serve as a couple.

Serving as a husband-and-wife team is a great way
to increase your effectiveness to the body of Christ.
Each of you brings special gifts, abilities, and experiences together as a couple. Find out what ministries in your church could use you as a team. Is it
the youth or children's ministry? The seniors? The
nursery during one of the church services? And
here's another idea: How about in place of your
next vacation, planning and preparing to take a
short-term, two-week summer missions trip?
That's sacrificial service...and an adventure to
boot! Service to the Lord and His people has its
own rewards, but serving together makes your service twice as fulfilling. And twice as fun, too!

3. Encourage your wife in her service.

Your wife is a wonderful person. She has her own
unique set of spiritual gifts, abilities, and talents.
She has a caring heart and a giving spirit, and she
doesn't want to jeopardize her priorities of being a
wife and mother. Therefore she may be reluctant to
serve outside the home. You are a fortunate man to
have such a remarkable and godly wife. But she has
so much to offer the body of Christ and your
church—her spiritual giftedness, her generous
heart, her organizational mind, and her special talents. Continue to help her keep her life in balance

and, without endangering her roles of wife and mother, encourage her to find an area of service. How can you encourage your wife in her service this week? Plan for the two of you to talk about it soon, but in the meantime...

1. Volunteer to take care of the children while she helps out at the Saturday women's seminar.

2. Give reinforcement to her desire to teach a women's or children's class.

3. Give direction as she develops her spiritual gifts.

4. Give praise and prayer support as she steps out in ministry.

5. Be an example of selfless service yourself. This will be her greatest encouragement...and model!

4. Be faithful in the "little things."

What's nice about serving is that you can start serving today—that's a "little thing." You don't need any training to start serving the Lord. It's a "little thing" to sweep the floors at church, pick up after the Sunday service, help with repairs around the church. None of these "little things" requires a six-week training class. So start serving in the "little things."

And, as you grow in your faith and get a better understanding of your spiritual gifts and are faithful in your service in the "little things," you will also grow in your capability for service. With that increased capacity may come the need for further training. (This is where the six-week class comes in!) But your service to the Lord and His people all starts with being faithful in the "little things." Isn't that what Jesus said the progression would be? "Well done, good and faithful servant; you were faithful over a few things, I will make you ruler over many things" (Matthew 25:21).

12

Reaching Out
to Others

*You shall be witnesses to Me
in Jerusalem, and in all Judea and Samaria,
and to the end of the earth.*
ACTS 1:8

Someone once asked a businessman, "What is your occupation?"

"I am a Christian," was the man's answer.

"No, I think you misunderstood me," said the inquirer. "I mean what is your job?"

The answer was the same. "I'm a Christian."

With a hint of frustration, the man persisted. "What I meant to say was, what do you do for a living?"

"My full-time occupation is to be a Christian, but I am an accountant to pay my living expenses," was the reply.

How would you respond to the question, "What is your occupation?"? For most Christian men, the answer would be to state what they do to "pay my living expenses."

Now, you may be wondering why I am concluding a book about marriage with a chapter on reaching out to others. Well, as you know, we have been looking at 12 things that really matter in the life of a husband after God's heart. And I can't think of a more important activity for a man of God than that of reaching out to others with the good news of Jesus Christ. Consider this thought: When you and your dear wife join hands...hearts...and feet...to take the good news to others, it is a doubly rewarding experience. I recently read a list of suggestions for couples entitled "What Draws Us Closer to God?" One of the suggestions listed was "sharing your faith."[20] That's good news in itself! And if there was ever a need for some good news, it is today. The world is full of bad news. I recently read an article that had the headline, BAD NEWS: GOOD-NEWSPAPER DIES FOR LACK OF MATERIAL. The article began,

> As you may have seen, the "good-news" paper in California recently folded because the editors found that there just wasn't enough good news to fill it. The paper couldn't even print its own obituary because that, of course, was bad news.[21]

> Pray that as you model Christlike behavior before others, they will respond to God.

And why is the news of Jesus "good news"? It is good news because Jesus' death for our sins offers freedom... freedom from guilt, freedom from loneliness, freedom from a meaningless life, and freedom from death—spiritual death. Now, that's good news! In the words of the apostle Paul, "How beautiful are the feet of those who bring good news!" (Romans 10:15 NIV). And whose feet are better to take this good news to your loved ones, your neighbors, and your acquaintances than those belonging to you and your wife?

Bringing the Good News

At this point, I'm assuming that you have experienced the good news of Jesus Christ in your own life—that you have experienced God's freedom from guilt, loneliness, meaninglessness, and death. If my assumptions are wrong and you are not yet a child of God, you should reread page 32. Perhaps now is the time you will experience God's freedom through His Son, Jesus Christ. What a radical change that will make in you, your marriage, and your life!

So let's talk now about your real occupation—that of being a Christian and the joy you can have in bringing God's good news to those around you. The joy of sharing about your salvation is reinforced by this mandate from your Savior:

> You shall be witnesses to Me in Jerusalem, and in all Judea and Samaria, and to the end of the earth (Acts 1:8).

Jesus Himself instructed His early disciples to be His witnesses, and He has extended that instruction to you and me too. For the early followers of Christ, that path of witness was to start locally in the city of Jerusalem. Then it was to expand to the entire country of Judea. Next, to the neighboring region of Samaria. And finally, to the ends of the earth. And friend, these are our marching orders today as well. We are to be Jesus' witnesses in *our* Jerusalem, in *our* Judea, in *our* Samaria, and to *our* world. And who are the people we are to reach with this good news?

Reaching Out to Your Wife

Fellow husband, we have spent this entire book talking about reaching out to your wife, haven't we? We have learned that next to your relationship with God, your closest relationship is to be with your wife. You are to love your wife sacrificially (Ephesians 5:25). You are to live with her in an understanding way and hold her in the highest honor (1 Peter 3:7). You are to never forget that God is asking you to esteem her and look out for her interests, even at the expense of your own (Philippians 2:3-4). And you are to humbly serve her (Galatians 5:13).

But what if your wife is not a believer? In that case you should work doubly hard on your marriage and pray twice as much for your wife and her salvation. Keep in mind that your marriage, whether to a believer or an unbeliever, is a sacred trust from God. You made a vow before God and witnesses that you would commit to living out all the things we have talked about in this book. And, friend, it doesn't matter how bad things get at home. You are still to lovingly reach out to your wife. God's Word says, "If any brother has a wife who does not believe, and she is willing to live with him, let him not divorce her" (1 Corinthians 7:12).

Sharing a Word of Testimony

Reaching out to an unbelieving wife was my story for the first eight years of my marriage. When I met my wife-to-be,

I was not walking with the Lord. Elizabeth was sweet, pretty, and intelligent. And believe it or not, she liked me! I fell madly in love with this southern beauty...and eight months after our first date, we were married. There was only one problem—she was not a Christian! And as you would expect, those eight years of married life had their ups and downs. As the joke goes, "If a child of God marries a child of the devil, said child of God is sure to have some trouble with his father-in-law!"

But God is faithful even when we are unfaithful and faithless (2 Timothy 2:13). One day while I was in a medical clinic as a pharmaceutical salesman, a faithful Christian doctor gave me a book. He was so excited about its contents that he handed me the book in his office while we were talking. I (as a good salesman) wanted to be able to discuss the contents of the book the next time I visited his office, so I immediately read all of it. The truths presented about Jesus Christ in that book really got me to thinking about my spiritual life and how far off-track I was. As soon as I finished the book, I gave it to Elizabeth, hoping she would read it. Well, two years later she finally got around to reading it. And when she was confronted with the facts about the person of Jesus Christ, she became a Christian—praise God!

Realizing the Importance of Reaching Out

Do you yet realize the importance of reaching out? One faithful doctor whose real occupation was that of being a Christian reached out to me (and to many others). He was very up-front about his faith. Everyone who came into his office was treated to Christian literature, Christian music, and Christian love, both from him and his senior nurse, whose occupation was also that of being a Christian. Then I reached out to Elizabeth. Then together we purchased ten copies of that same book and passed them out to as many people as we knew at that time. And now we both reach out to others every day.

Do you also see the importance of reaching out to an unsaved wife? Maybe this applies to you. Maybe you came to Christ after you and your wife married. If so, that means you have changed, but she is still in spiritual "darkness" (1 Peter 2:9). To you, my friend, I say do as I did. Ask your wife to read a Christian book, and be willing to read along with her. And then pray that she will respond positively to the truth she is reading—as my wife did. Ask her to attend church with you or go "church shopping" together with you on Sundays, followed by a nice brunch or lunch afterward. Make it a special time. And pray! Pray that God will send others who will reach out to her with His life-changing truth and good news. Pray that God will use your changed life to reach her as He has reached you through others. Pray that as you model Christlike behavior before her, she will respond to God. And above all, don't ever give up! Keep praying and keep reaching out, no matter what!

Now you may be saying, "This doesn't apply to me because my wife is a believer." If that's the case, then brother, thank God daily for a wife who knows and loves the Lord. I have experienced marriage without and with a believing wife, and I thank God every day for the transformation in our marriage because of Jesus Christ. So, as I've repeated often throughout this book, don't ever take your loving wife for granted. Make sure you are constantly expressing your appreciation to her and cultivating your marriage relationship.

Reaching Out to Your Children

Many married Christian men are blessed with a wife who is a strong and growing Christian. Her desire is to be a godly wife and mother. And because she is such a knowledgeable and dedicated Christian, the husband tends to delegate the spiritual education of the children to her.

But, fellow husband, this is not God's design for a husband and father. Again, thank God for your faithful Christian wife, but realize that God's Word says you are to be involved in every effort to reach out to their children and "bring them up in the training and admonition of the Lord" (Ephesians 6:4). Fathers are also to reach out and warn their children against evil—"My son, hear the instruction of your father" (Proverbs 1:8). And it was a father who gave this advice: "My son, if you receive my words, and treasure my commands within you, so that you incline your ear to wisdom, and apply your heart to understanding... then you will understand the fear of the LORD" (Proverbs 2:1-2,5).

As I reflect back on my parenting days, I can only thank God for His grace. Because of my responsibilities at church and my involvement in overseas pastoral training, I was gone a lot. But whenever I was at home I made it a priority to have breakfast and devotions with my family. And even if I was going out in the evening for ministry, I would schedule that ministry for later in the evening so I could have dinner with my family. And definitely one of the most special times for me as a father was tucking my little ones into bed each night, talking about their day, and praying with each one as they drifted off to sleep. Then, as they grew older, my girls and I would have special "coke dates."

It was on these "dates"—when emotions were calm and things could be looked at objectively—that I helped each of them to write out what the Bible said they should look for in a "guy friend." Later their lists became important documents God used in their lives...all because I made it a priority to "be there" as much as I could and to be vitally involved with my daughters whenever possible.

I know you are busy, and I know you have a lot of options competing for your time. But spending as much time as you can with your children will give you life's greatest joys and blessings. So I urge you to make time with your children a major priority. Talk constantly with them about the Lord. Relate everything in your life to your Christian faith. Christian father, *you* are the best representative of Christ to your children. Let them see you live it out. Let them enjoy and relish the gift of your presence and attention. Let them have long, sustained looks at what a Christian looks like. Don't expect your children to embrace your faith and make it their own until they have witnessed the strength of your faith and your trust in God.

> Every time you and your wife reach out to others, it draws the two of you closer to each other...and to God.

And here are a few other "musts" for reaching out to your children. Pray with and for your children. Take them to church each week. Teach them God's Word and the gospel message through devotional times and bedtime reading. Be their best friend...because you can talk to a friend about anything, including Jesus Christ! Then, Lord willing, one day your children will relate everything in their life to *their* Christian faith. While children crave your attention, make sure you, dear fellow father, take advantage of the very few short years God gives you to reach out to them while they are still under your roof.

Reaching Out to Your Neighbors

Unless you live in a remote part of Montana or some other unpopulated region, you probably have neighbors. But in our busy, fast-paced world, it's easy to ignore them. You come and go, with maybe a hand-wave or a hello that you weakly offer over the hedge or fence separating your two houses. Is this what the Bible means when it says to "love...your neighbor as yourself" (Luke 10:27)? I think not. You must realize God has sovereignly placed you in your neighborhood. You must see your neighborhood as your most significant mission field.

Here's a question for you: What would you do if you were a missionary in a foreign country who desired to reach out to others with the gospel of Jesus Christ? You would start building relationships with your neighbors so that someday you might be able to share about salvation through Jesus with them, wouldn't you? Well, guess what? You don't have to go to a foreign country to serve as a missionary and a witness. You are a missionary to the people next door. And you don't even have to learn a foreign language! So team up with your wife and make an effort to reach out to your neighbors. Pray as a family for your neighbors by name. Invite them into your home. Allow them to observe your marriage and your family life.

This is what happened to Bob and Terry. They lived two doors down from Elizabeth and me. We put them on our prayer list, reached out to them, and befriended them. We had them in our home on many occasions. One day Bob asked me to share with him about our child-raising "philosophy." It was then that I began to expose Bob to what the Bible has to say about raising children...and a lot of other things as well! It wasn't too many months before Bob and Terry and their three boys were going to church with us. And it wasn't long after that when the whole family became Christians. Praise God!

It's true that most of your neighbors will not purposefully "darken the doors" of a church where they might hear the message of the Bible. Therefore you need to take the church and its message to them. In fact, you are the only Bible that some of your neighbors will ever read. Make sure that when you are with your neighbors you do more than just "small talk" and do your part to reach out with God's message of salvation.

> You talk about the weather,
>
>> And the crops of corn and wheat;
>
> You speak of friends and neighbors
>
>> That pass along the street;
>
> You call yourself a Christian,
>
>> And like the gospel plan—
>
> Then why not speak of Jesus,
>
>> And speak out like a man?[22]

Reaching Out on the Job

Remember my doctor friend who reached out to me with a book? Well, witnessing on the job can be as easy as giving a fellow worker a book or a gospel tract or pamphlet. It can also be as natural as sharing your testimony. If you are a Christian, you have a testimony. Your testimony is your story of how you became a Christian. What's great about your testimony is that it's your personal story of how you met the Savior, so no one can refute it. You should always be prepared to share it, and you should always be enthusiastic about doing so! Here is a simple three-step method someone gave me to help develop my personal story, my testimony. Basically this allows you to tell your story in three simple parts:

Part 1—"How I lived my life before Christ." Share your background and what you thought about God, religion, and the Bible. Mention what characterized your life, such as loneliness, depression, greed, obsession with career, and so on, and how these affected your life.

Part 2—"How I met Jesus." Share how you became a Christian. If it's a little hard for you to convey your experience, you may want to use a good tract or small booklet that describes your relationship with Jesus.

Part 3—"How my life has changed since I met Jesus." Share how your thoughts about God, religion, and the Bible have changed. Also tell how your relationship with Jesus changed your marriage, your family life, your attitudes, and your desires.

Now, how do you get started in reaching out on the job? Simply ask God every day to open your eyes to the opportunities that are available to you to reach out and share your testimony with your workmates. Then open your mouth and "speak out like a man"!

> You talk about your business,
>
> > Your bonds and stocks and gold;
>
> And in all worldly matters
>
> > You are so brave and bold.
>
> But why are you so silent
>
> > About salvation's plan?
>
> Why don't you speak for Jesus,
>
> > And speak out like a man?[23]

Reaching Out to the World

More than likely you will never be a missionary in a far-away country. But that shouldn't stop you and your family from reaching out to the world in numerous ways. (And remember, every time you and your wife reach out to others, you'll be drawn closer to each other...and to God!) You can...

- ∞ Give of your finances to support missions.

- ∞ Pray for the missionaries your church supports.

- ∞ Have missionaries in your home.

- Pick a country and pray for the salvation of its people.

- Go on a summer missions trip.

- Participate in your church's outreach projects (especially at Christmastime).

Truly, this list could go on and on! It's like Jesus said—you are to be His witness "to the end of the earth"! That's a lifelong calling you and your wife and family are to work out every day...to the end of your days.

> I'd like to tell the story sweet
>
> Of Jesus, wouldn't you?
>
> To help some other folks to meet
>
> Their Savior, wouldn't you?
>
> I'd like to travel all the way
>
> To where I'd hear my Jesus say:
>
> "You've helped My work along today."
>
> I'd like that. Wouldn't you?[24]

Wrapping Up What Really Matters in Your Marriage

This chapter has been about reaching out to others with the life-saving, life-changing message of salvation. And I hope you will give much thought and prayer to God's assignment of reaching out to those He has placed in your circle of relationships. And I pray that you are planning to take immediate action.

But this is also the end of our book about being a husband after God's own heart. I'm sure that as you have read along with me, many of the chapters served as a review and reminder of the things that really matter in your marriage. But I also hope there were "things" that gave you food for thought and "things" for you to work on and change. Being a husband after God's own heart may at times be a daunting task, but it is a task God Himself is asking you to fulfill.

As we come to the close of our time together, I have one final word for you—Don't let yourself become discouraged about the task. God will help you. Godly men can help you, and hopefully this book will help you. I have written this entire volume out of a heart of prayer for you, praying that you would be encouraged, motivated, and stimulated by its message and excited about the many practical "little things" you can do to live out your role as a husband. There is hope—*great* hope—because God has given you all the resources you need to accomplish the task, everything that you need to fulfill His will and design for you as a husband (2 Peter 1:3). And, blessing upon blessings, God has also promised to give you the full strength of His enabling power and His all-sufficient wisdom and grace (2 Corinthians 12:9) to be a godly leader in your marriage and family...and to be a husband after His own heart.

Little Things That Make a Big Difference

1. Open your home.

One of the easiest ways for you and your wife to reach out to others is by inviting others into your home. Invite your neighbors in for dessert. Invite your workmates over for dinner. This is your family's opportunity to further demonstrate the reality of Jesus Christ to those who know you. It's one thing for people to see your Christian life in the workplace or out in the yard, but it's so much more when they can see Christianity at work in your home.

The home is where your testimony can be seen in new ways. Just count the many blessings that God has given you as avenues to share your faith with others! For instance, He has given you a loving and faithful wife. He has given you wonderful and well-behaved children (...well, at least wonderful children). He has blessed you with a neat and comfortable home that radiates the peace of God. So inviting people into your home is a powerful way to reach out to your workmates and your neighbors. Make sure you and your wife agree on how—and how often—to open up your home. Then begin to pray for those special people God wants to bring into His "showcase"—your home and your hearts. Who does He want you to invite so they can experience

Christ's love through the hospitality that you and your wife provide?

2. Pray for a heart of compassion.

Compassion is not a very "manly" emotion, is it? Your wife can have compassion, but not you! Yet is compassion to be exhibited only by women? You know the answer to that, don't you? As always, Jesus is our example of a man who demonstrated compassion. He showed compassion for the sick. He wept over the inhabitants of Jerusalem because of their unbelief (Luke 19:41). He wept for his friend Lazarus (John 11:35). How are you doing in the Compassion Department? When was the last time you wept for the salvation of a loved one or a workmate or neighbor? If compassion is not one of your strengths (which it should be, as a man and a husband after God's own heart), then begin to pray for God to soften your heart.

3. Participate in neighborhood activities.

You have a wonderful opportunity to reach out to your neighbors by just being a "good neighbor." So make sure you and your family participate in neighborhood yard sales, block parties, your Neighborhood Watch program. Volunteer to feed your neighbors' pets while they go on vacation. Pick up their mail and bring in their newspapers. Water their lawn. None of these activities requires you to say one word about your beliefs. But your joyful spirit and servant attitude will speak volumes about your faith. Hopefully as you give, expecting and asking nothing in return (Luke 6:35), your neighbors will want to know more about why you are so different. Then you can share your beliefs with them. Who knows what God will do in their hearts?

4. Invite your acquaintances to church.

Your local church is God's gift to you and your family, but it is also God's gift to a lost world. Just as you and your family are blessed by the programs that are offered at your church, your neighbors and workmates can receive a blessing from them as well. Don't be shy. Be excited about what's going on at your church. Share that enthusiasm with others. They need the saving hand of Jesus. And your church is just the place where they might meet the Savior. Invite the neighborhood children to youth activities. Invite their parents to seminars on parenting and marriage. Take them with you to a family or couples' retreat. You do the praying and inviting, and let God do the rest!

5. Give a book or tract.

Have you read a Christian book that has been helpful in your marriage or with your children or on your job or with your finances? Then give that same book to an acquaintance. These books address certain practical subjects in life, but they also speak to the real issue in life—a relationship with Jesus Christ. So give these books, trusting God to use the principles in them to speak to the hearts of the recipients. In His timing and in His way, God can prompt your friends and neighbors to read the books. Just be sure to make the books available!

Study Questions

Chapter 1—Growing in the Lord

1. What is your most common excuse or rationale for not having time for spiritual growth, and how does it hold up to the truth of Matthew 6:33?

2. How do you think the three verses in Psalm 119:9-11 could help a husband with temptation, and what truths does 1 Corinthians 10:12-13 add for promoting purity?

3. Read both Ephesians 4:13-14 and Hebrews 5:12-14. Then jot down two ways you can grow in wisdom and discernment.

4. What impressed you most about Joshua, and which one area of the four areas of greatness in his life will you pursue?

5. Because growing in the Lord really matters in your marriage, what one "little thing" can you do this week to promote your growth in the Lord?

Chapter 2—Working as a Team

1. Read 1 Corinthians 13:11 and apply it to the concept of a "team" in marriage. Can you point to any "childish things" you need to put away?

2. Read Genesis 3:1-6. For whatever reason, Eve "did battle" with the enemy without her husband's help. In what ways are you available for your wife's spiritual needs? Are there any ways that you are not available and should be?

3. Read again the questions under the section "Back to the Basics." Which questions do you need to revisit and work on to make yours a more "perfect" marriage?

4. Because working as a team really matters in your marriage, what one "little thing" can you do this week to bring you two closer together as a team?

Chapter 3—Learning to Communicate

1. In your Bible, look up the verses below. Then evaluate your communication skills and the qualities mentioned in each verse, based on a scale of...

> <u>doing well</u> or
> <u>needs improvement</u> or
> <u>not good at all</u>

Swift in your listening—Proverbs 18:2

Prudent in your words—Proverbs 10:19

Edifying with your approach—Ephesians 4:29

Empathetic in your voice—Proverbs 15:1

Calming every issue—Proverbs 16:21

Honoring the truth with your words—Ephesians 4:25

2. Now what one major step will you take to begin improving your communication with your wife?

3. Glance again at the hindrances to good communication. Which one is your biggest problem? Can you think of any solutions or ways to "turn a corner"? Jot them down.

4. Because learning to communicate really matters in your marriage, what one "little thing" will you do this week to more effectively communicate with your wife?

Chapter 4—Enjoying Intimacy

1. If you have a dictionary handy, look up the word *intimacy*. What strikes you most as you think about this word in connection with your relationship with your wife?

2. One of the most important verses in the Bible for a husband is 1 Peter 3:7. Look at it in your Bible. In what ways is a wife "weaker" than her husband? In what ways, then, can or must a husband be strong for his wife? Or, put another way, how can you come alongside your wife and help?

3. As you think about sexual intimacy with your wife, what information do these scriptures provide?

  Genesis 2:25

  1 Corinthians 7:1-5

  Hebrews 13:4

4. When it comes to your conduct toward women other than your wife, what instruction do these scriptures give you?

  Job 31:1

  Proverbs 5:15-19

  Malachi 2:15

  Matthew 5:27-28

What steps can a husband take to follow these instructions from God?

5. Because enjoying intimacy really matters in your marriage, what one "little thing" can you do this week to enhance intimacy with your wife?

Chapter 5—Managing Your Money

1. Do you agree or disagree with Dr. Graham's statement about a person's attitude about money? Why or why not?

2. As an eye-opener, look at your checkbook and credit card statements for last month. What do they reveal about your interests, hobbies, spending habits, and giving practices?

3. Read 2 Corinthians 8:1-4 in your Bible. As you consider the three ways you are to approach giving to your church and other Christian concerns—appropriate, sacrificial, and voluntary—in which areas do you excel and/or fall short? Are there any changes you need to make?

4. Glance again at the section entitled "Money Matters in Marriage." How do you think the three "wrong" attitudes toward money—covetousness, idolatry, and

worldliness—can create tension and conflict in a marriage?

5. Which one of the activities from the letters of L-E-A-D-E-R can you attempt this week?

6. Because managing your money really matters in your marriage, what one "little thing" can you do this week to better manage your money?

Chapter 6—Keeping Up the Home

1. Do you agree or disagree that your home is a reflection of your religion? Why or why not? What do you think others are seeing of your "religion" when they look at your home?

2. Review these verses and "perspectives" in your Bible.

   Wisdom—Proverbs 24:3-4
   Godliness—Proverbs 15:6
   Leadership—1 Timothy 3:5
   Care—Proverbs 24:30-31

Which areas need more of your attention, and why?

3. Scan through the "Problems...and Solutions" presented in this chapter. Which category of husband do you most closely resemble? What can you do to turn things around and be more committed to keeping up your home?

4. Because keeping up the home really matters in your marriage, what one "little thing" can you do this week on your house?

Chapter 7—Raising Your Children

1. After thinking about the opening story and the principles of "Parenting 101," evaluate your relationship to your children in the areas that follow. Where are you strongest, and where are you weakest? Note one improvement you can make in each area.

   Instruction—
   Showing love for God—
   Consistent Christian environment—
   Time—
   Discipline—
   Example—

2. Time—there never seems to be enough of it! What advice does Ephesians 5:15-17 give you about your approach to time?

How does this wisdom regarding "time" relate to raising your children?

How does this wisdom regarding your "walk" relate to raising your children?

3. Because raising your children really matters in your marriage, what one "little thing" can you do this week for or with your children?

Chapter 8—Extending Love to Family
1. What does Exodus 20:12 instruct you to do?

And what is the promise for obeying this commandment, according to Ephesians 6:2-3?

2. In your Bible, scan through Exodus 4:18 and 18:1-27, which tell the story of Moses and Jethro. Then answer these questions:

How do I show humility to my parents and in-laws?

What have I done recently to honor my parents and in-laws?

How often do I communicate with my parents and in-laws?

Would I consider my parents and in-laws to be my friends? Why or why not?

Do I ask for advice and do I listen to my parents and in-laws? Why or why not?

3. Which hindrances have you been guilty of using as excuses in your relationship with your parents and in-laws, and what steps can you take to overcome these barriers?

Distance

Absence

Selfishness

Manipulation

4. Because extending love to family really matters in your marriage, what one "little thing" can you do this week to improve your relationship with your extended family?

Chapter 9—Tending Your Career

1. In what ways do you identify with "Joe" in his initial attitude about his job?

2. Now look in your Bible at the teachings that changed Joe's attitude toward his job. What insight does each of these truths give you about your job?

   Colossians 3:23—

   Ephesians 6:5-7—

   1 Corinthians 10:31—

3. Under the section "Doing God's Will," which element listed below is presently the most helpful in shaping your attitude about your job? And which of these elements do you need to give a more prominent position in your thinking and in your performance on the job?

Perceiving God's will—

Providing for your family—

Proving to be a servant—

Proclaiming your faith—

Pursuing your career—

4. How would you rate your level of contentment in relation to your job? What might be some of the reasons for your dissatisfaction? Do you lack purpose, understanding, or obedience? How will you remedy this?

5. Did you follow through and answer the questions dealing with balance in your life? If not, do so now. If you did, what one major change can you make so you reap more abundant blessings from your work?

6. Because tending your career really matters in your marriage, what one "little thing" can you do this week about your career?

Chapter 10—Making Time for Fun

1. Describe the last time you and your wife went out together, just the two of you. What made it fun?

2. Your relationship with God and your position in Christ should bring great joy to you, joy that can be shared with your wife. What sources of joy are available to you, according to these passages?

   Galatians 5:22—

   Nehemiah 8:10—

3. How does the Bible say your joy—or lack of it—affects others, according to...

   ...Proverbs 15:13?

   ...Proverbs 15:15?

   ...Proverbs 17:22?

4. Briefly look again at "What Happened to the Fun?" Which one of the "cares" listed there has contributed the most to robbing joy from your marriage? Can you think of one change you can make immediately?

5. Have you asked others, including your wife, for suggestions of fun things to do as a couple? If you have, list several here. If not, do so this week.

   —   —

   —   —

6. Because making time for fun really matters in your marriage, what one "little thing" can you do this week to add a little fun to your marriage?

Chapter 11—Serving the Lord

1. Do you know a couple who faithfully and wholeheartedly serve the Lord? Take a minute to jot down what you appreciate about their commitment to serving the Lord. Also note a few of the things they do in their service to others.

2. Read Ephesians 2:10 in your Bible. What does this verse say about your service to the Lord? And how does—or should—this affect your attitude toward your service to God's people?

3. Now read Joshua 24:15. How does Joshua's heart for serving God serve as an example for you and your house and your commitment to serve the Lord? Are there any changes you must make? Note them here.

4. If you are already actively serving God's people, what advice would you give a man who asks you, "How can I begin to serve?" Or, if you are the man who's asking, "How can I begin to serve?" what did you learn in this chapter about some first steps you can take?

5. What did you admire most about Aquila and Priscilla, and how can you and your wife begin to emulate this noble couple who faithfully served the Lord and His people?

6. List here the three responses husbands are most likely to make when it comes to service in the church. Then circle the one you consider yourself to be at this

time...and the one you desire to be. How can you begin to serve with all your heart?

—   —   —

7. Because serving the Lord really matters in your marriage, what one "little thing" can you do this week?

Chapter 12—Reaching Out to Others

1. Describe how others reached out to you with the saving message of Jesus Christ before you became a Christian. While you're at it, offer a prayer of thanksgiving to God for sending those wonderful people into your life. And if you want to go a step further, write each one of them a note of gratitude.

2. Look at Acts 1:8 in your Bible. What people do you consider to be your...

...Jerusalem?

...Judea?

...Samaria?

...ends of the earth?

Place these people's names on a 3" x 5" card and ask God to begin guiding you in ways to reach out to them.

3. There's nothing quite like being prepared. So here's an assignment for this next week: On a sheet of paper, write out your answers to the three parts of your testimony (see the section entitled "Reaching Out on the Job" on pages 205-206). Begin asking God for opportunities to share your testimony with others.

4. Under the section entitled "Reaching Out to the World," select one project you and your family can participate in. What will that project be? And what first step can you take on the selected project this week?

5. Because reaching out to others really matters in your marriage, what one "little thing" can you do this week to reach out?

Notes

1. Charles R. Swindoll, *The Tale of the Tardy Oxcart,* quoting Wayne Martindale, *The Quotable Lewis* (Nashville: Word Publishing, 1998), p. 468.

2. Jim George, *A Man After God's Own Heart* (Eugene, OR: Harvest House Publishers, 2002).

3. Gary Thomas, *Sacred Marriage* (Grand Rapids: Zondervan, 2000), p. 77.

4. John MacArthur, *The MacArthur Study Bible* (Nashville: Word Publishing, 1979), p. 21.

5. Roy B. Zuck, *The Speaker's Quote Book,* quoting Les Cantrell (Grand Rapids: Kregel Publications, 1997), p. 78.

6. Ibid.

7. Stuart Scott, *The Exemplary Husband* (Bemidji, MN: Focus Publishing, Inc., 2000), p. 227.

8. Ibid., p. 106.

9. Charles F. Pfeiffer and Everett F. Harrison, eds., *The Wycliffe Bible Commentary* (Chicago: Moody Press, 1990), p. 938.

10. Alice Gray, *Lists to Live By,* The First Colection, quoting Claudia and David Arp (Sisters, OR: Multnomah Publishers, 1999), p. 137.

11. *Checklist for Life for Men* (Nashville: Thomas Nelson Publishers, 2002), p. 77.

12. Ibid., p. 169.

13. John MacArthur, *The MacArthur Study Bible,* p. 1862.

14. Steve Farrar, *Point Man—How a Man Can Lead His Family* (Sisters, OR: Multnomah Publishers, Inc., 1990), p. 202.

15. Hans Finzel, *Help! I'm a Baby Boomer* (Wheaton, IL: Victor Books, 1989), p. 61.

16. Ibid.

17. Michael Griffith, *God's Forgetful Pilgrims: Recalling the Church to Its Reason for Being* (Grand Rapids: Eerdmans, 1975).

18. J. Oswald Sanders, *Spiritual Leadership* (Chicago: Moody Press, 1970), p. 59.

19. Priscilla and Aquila are mentioned in Acts 18:1-3,18-19,26; 1 Corinthians 16:19; Romans 16:3-5.

20. Alice Gray, *Lists to Live by for Every Married Couple* (Sisters, OR: Multnomah Publishers, 2001), p. 30.

21. Arthur G. McPhee, *Friendship Evangelism—the Caring Way to Share Your Faith* (Grand Rapids: Zondervan Publishing House, 1978), p. 17.

22. Eleanor L. Doan, *The Speaker's Sourcebook*, "Speak Out for Jesus"—author unknown (Grand Rapids, MI: Zondervan Publishing House, 1977), p. 284.

23. Ibid.

24. Ibid.

Personal Notes

Personal Notes

_____

_____

_____

_____

_____

_____

_____

_____

_____

_____

_____

_____

_____

_____

_____

_____

_____

_____

Personal Notes

_____

_____

_____

_____

_____

_____

_____

_____

_____

_____

_____

_____

_____

_____

_____

_____

Personal Notes

Personal Notes

$\mathcal{D}$ouble the benefits of *A Husband After God's Own Heart* by giving your wife the companion volume

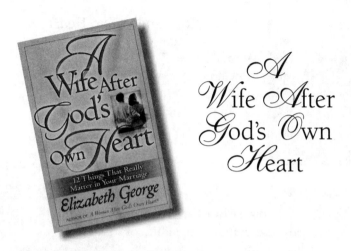

A Wife After God's Own Heart

This book by Elizabeth George is rich with practical insights and guidance that will bring greater mutual love, friendship, romance, and happiness to your marriage.

Elizabeth George has also written *A Wife After God's Own Heart Growth and Study Guide,* which provides additional personal applications and is great for individual and group use.

Books by Jim and Elizabeth George are
available at your local Christian bookstore
or can be ordered from:

Jim and Elizabeth George Ministries
P.O. Box 2879
Belfair, WA 98528
Toll-free fax/phone: 1-800-542-4611
www.JimGeorge.com

Other Books by Jim George

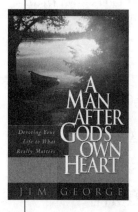

A Man After God's Own Heart
Many Christian men want to be men after God's own heart...but how do they do this? George shows that a heartfelt desire to practice God's priorities is all that's needed. God's grace does the rest.

God's Man of Influence
How can a man have a life of lasting impact? Here are the secrets to having a positive and meaningful influence in the lives of everyone a man meets, including his own wife and children.

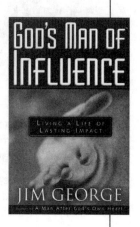

God's Wisdom for Little Boys
(coauthored with Elizabeth George)
The wonderful teachings of Proverbs come to life for boys. Memorable rhymes play alongside colorful watercolors for a charming presentation of truths to live by.